United Counties

Kevin Lane

Front cover: Bristol FLF6B/ECW 623 (YNV 623), new in December 1961, leaves the stand in Bridge Street, Luton, on 19 January 1974, bound for Leighton Buzzard via Dunstable, Hockliffe and Eggington. This section of Bridge Street is no longer served by buses, while the Co-op store has given way to a cinema complex. *Chris Lodington*

Back cover: Bedford bus station in October 1967, with a variety of Bristol/ECW types. Prominent, having worked in from Biggleswade, is K5G 830 (FRP 684) of 1952, while alongside, having arrived from Aylesbury, is LD6B 525 (ORP 25) of 1957; on the far left is LS6B coach 482 (JBD 486) of 1954, while just visible on the right is KSW5G 876 (SHK 519), one of the newest vehicles inherited from Eastern National in 1952. *Mike Sutcliffe*

Title page: United Counties received its first rear-engined double-deckers in 1969 in the form of ECW-bodied Bristol VRTSLs. Deliveries of the type would continue throughout the 1970s; 774 (ANV 774J), a Series 2 model, is pictured while on layover in Oxford's Gloucester Green bus station when new in 1971. *Author's collection*

Contents

First published 2005

ISBN (10) 0 7110 3081 2
ISBN (13) 978 0 7110 3081 7

Published by Ian Allan Publishing

an imprint of Ian Allan Publishing Ltd, Hersham, Surrey KT12 4RG. Printed in England by Ian Allan Printing Ltd, Hersham, Surrey KT12 4RG.

Visit the Ian Allan Publishing website at www.ianallanpublishing.com

Code: 0509/B1

On New Year's Day 1965 (not a public holiday in those days) Bristol LS5G 452 (HNV 730) disturbs the peace at Ashwell, Church End, working a Royston–Hitchin journey on route 91. *Tony Moyes*

Introduction

Look at a map of major UK bus operators and it will be apparent that the majority of BET and Tilling companies served areas of interest to tourists and holidaymakers — somewhere to *go* rather than to pass through. As such, this tended to endear them to enthusiasts, some, like Southdown, East Kent, Devon General and Crosville, having a long-standing following (besides which buses at the seaside are always worth a second glance). There is even something a bit special about certain 'inland' companies, the peculiarities of the home-made buses of Midland Red and the attractive red and duck-egg blue of City of Oxford working beneath the 'dreaming spires', not to mention the bleak moorland terrain traversed by characterful Bristol L5Gs of North Western Road Car. And then there were the coaches; who could fail to be captivated by Black & White Motorways, Royal Blue or a Ribble 'White Lady'?

There are a few other companies that had none of this glamour, what I would call 'bread and butter' operations. Amongst these I would include the likes of Yorkshire Traction, East Midland and (I'll get to it eventually), United Counties, whose traditional area was Northamptonshire. It all started in Wellingborough, gradually expanding throughout the county, particularly during the 1930s, when so many small and not so small independents threw in the towel. Further expansion took the company south into Buckinghamshire, whilst express operations to London from Nottingham and Oxford, not to mention their involvement with Associated Motorways gave a boost to its coaching activities. Following the transfer in May 1952 of Eastern National's Midland Area, which virtually doubled the size of the company, such exotic places as Bedford and Luton were also on the map!

So what qualifies United Counties for inclusion into the 'Glory Days' series? I suppose the easy answer is that it is worthy by virtue of being a solid, no-nonsense and workaday company and that relatively little has been written about it,

excluding the invaluable history written and published by Roger Warwick (see Bibliography). Certainly it has been under-photographed, except by those who live within its borders. I turned my camera towards it during the 1970s, while taking pictures of railways and wish I had taken more interest before the demise of the older types.

What actually constitutes the 'Glory Days' to a particular operator is always open to conjecture, although to concentrate only on, say, the 1950s, would produce a slim and imbalanced volume. I have taken the story of United Counties up to 1986, when it was carved up in the interests of selling it off to the private sector. This is, I know, rather late, and the rag-bag of clapped-out and second-hand vehicles hired or acquired during the first half of the 1970s was anything but glorious, but it is a convenient cut-off point, and there were a lot of interesting developments during the National Bus Company period. The past 20 years has also received an overview, not least

To many enthusiasts of a certain age the 1950s would represent the 'glory days' of United Counties, despite the fleet's almost wholly Tilling look by this time. An excuse, then, to include this view at the old Bedford bus station of Bristol KSW6B 969 (KNV 342) and KSW5G 921 (HNV 737) looking very much the part. *Peter Yeomans*

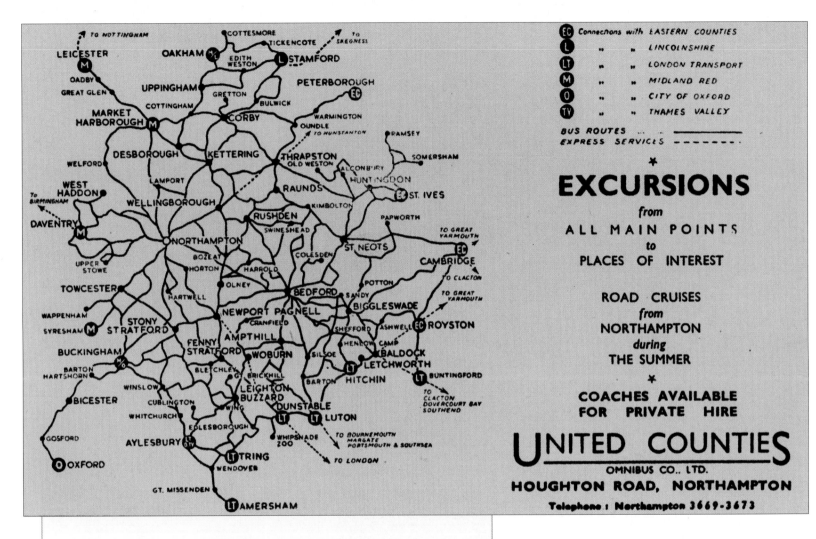

Map showing the extent of United Counties routes after the absorption of Eastern National's erstwhile Midland Area.

through a desire to include the Routemasters that plied their trade in Bedford and Corby for a few years, a period that certainly *was* glorious!

Thanks are due to the various photographers and others who have plundered their collections for pictures and other material and who have been individually credited. Particular thanks are due to Alan Parfitt, for his help and encouragement, and to Roger Warwick, who had the dedication to record the history of United Counties in such detail; this book would be much the poorer without it. Continued thanks are also due to Maureen, my wife, and to Andrew, my youngest son, for his help with guidance around the computer, this being my first book to be written using one!

Kevin Lane
Dunstable
May 2005

Much of the territory served by United Counties was quite rural in nature. Bristol LS5G 456 (HBD 636) works a 364 journey from Cheddington Green to Aylesbury through Long Marston in the late 1960s. *Author's collection*

Amongst the author's personal favourites were the five Plaxton-bodied Bristol RELH6L coaches of 1974. No 219 (SBD 219M) stands at London Victoria in February 1981 before working an evening 455 service back to Northampton. *Author*

1. Origins and Early Days

The United Counties story begins in Wellingborough, a small industrial town in Northamptonshire. However, the seeds were sown in London, where one William Benjamin Richardson had been running horse and then motor buses since 1895, having previously been a horse-bus driver. The London Central Motor Omnibus Co Ltd was formed in 1906 and in 1911 was renamed as the New Central Omnibus Co Ltd. The new title reflected the company's aspirations to expand outside the capital, and by May 1912 operations had commenced in Bedford, where it soon took over the Bedford Motor Omnibus Co.

It was later discovered that a New Central Omnibus driver and his conductor were hiring a bus each weekend and operating it in Wellingborough! As this turned out to be quite a profitable exercise, the management officially sent a bus and crew to work in the town from around 10 o'clock in the morning until late in the evening. This was operated initially as a circular service from Wellingborough to Rushden via Finedon, Irthlingborough and Higham Ferrers and return, although a second bus and crew were later sent to operate a service in the reverse direction as well. (It is interesting to note that a United Counties driver

received a suspended jail sentence in May 1988 for taking a Bristol VR from Wellingborough outstation and operating an unauthorised service in the town, running five minutes ahead of the regular service bus!) Transport links in the area at this time were principally in the hands of the railways; the Midland Railway ran from London and Bedford northwards through Wellingborough and Kettering, with a branch line from Wellingborough to Higham Ferrers, whilst the London & North Western Railway ran east–west, from Northampton to Peterborough.

In the meantime the New Central Omnibus Co had been leased to the London General Omnibus Co Ltd from 1 January 1913, and William Richardson later made the decision to consolidate his operations in Northamptonshire, incorporating the Wellingborough Motor Omnibus Co Ltd on 3 May 1913.

The first year of the new company saw the development of a number of services, the following being operated from Irthlingborough garage:

Wellingborough to Northampton
  (daily)
Rushden to Kettering via Irthlingborough (daily)
Wellingborough to Raunds (daily)
Wellingborough to Desborough via Kettering (daily)
Northampton to Kettering (daily)
Irthlingborough to Rushden via Wellingborough
  (Monday to Saturday)
Wellingborough to Irthlingborough, Higham Ferrers,
  Rushden and back to Wellingborough (Sundays)

During World War 1 services were generally reduced or withdrawn, and several chassis were requisitioned by the War Department. Nevertheless, a profit was returned throughout the war, as, indeed, it would be throughout the company's eight-year existence.

The buses operated were mainly Leylands, mostly of the ST and 36hp types. Bodies were supplied initially by Birch or Dodson, although from 1919 they were mainly built 'in house', at Irthlingborough. Prior to 1919 vehicles were identified by a single letter (and registration number, of course), whereas from 1919 the stock number consisted of a class letter and number. Livery was predominantly blue, with a primrose band and red wheels and chassis. It should be added that the original Birch body from A3 (LF 9967) survived for many years as a storeshed at Wellingborough Sewage Works and has subsequently been fitted to a suitably modified Leyland chassis; as such, the 'Wellingborough', superbly restored by Mike Sutcliffe, is a familiar sight at rallies.

By 1921 further expansion was envisaged, but the company was under-capitalised, a situation not uncommon in the industry, and the decision was taken to form a new company to take over

▲ Seen outside the Green Dragon in the village of Broughton, 'S' (LH 8977) was one of a pair of Leyland STs fitted with single-deck bodywork. New in 1914, they were sold after only a few months to a dealer, both later ending up in the fledgling Southdown fleet. *Mike Sutcliffe collection*

the assets of the Wellingborough Motor Omnibus Co Ltd; thus was formed the United Counties Omnibus & Road Transport Co Ltd, incorporated on 1 September and taking over with effect from 1 October. The actual title of the company recalls the original United Counties Omnibus Co, registered in May 1913 and in which William Richardson had an involvement, although it was never operational. The aforementioned assets included 37 buses (plus two under construction) and spares, a Leyland lorry, four cars, the depot at Irthlingborough (including body building facilities) and various other cottages and properties.

The first new buses for United Counties were mainly RAF-type Leylands. One bus added to stock in 1922 was a second-hand acquisition from Luck & Andrews, Kettering, in the shape of a Dodson-bodied Leyland G7 'Charabus' B15 (BD 209). The body, which could be converted and used as either a single-deck bus or a charabanc within minutes, was patented and exhibited at the Commercial Vehicle Exhibition at Olympia in October 1921. It seems that United Counties used it as a fixed saloon and removed it in 1927, to be sold as a shop and later a shed; like the Wellingborough body described above, it survived to be mounted on another suitable Leyland chassis by Mike Sutcliffe and is also a rally favourite.

Further Leylands were taken into stock right throughout the 1920s, bodied mainly by Dodson, Short, Leyland or the company itself. Towards the end of the decade came the first of a number of operator acquisitions by United Counties (no routes having been acquired with the Luck & Andrews Leyland). Summerley Bros of Desborough brought several local routes and two Lancia saloons in March 1928, whilst

S10 (BD 3476) was amongst the first buses bought new by United Counties in 1922. An RAF-type Leyland with company-built body carrying 52 passengers, it would remain in the fleet until 1929. *Ian Allan Library*

Large numbers of Leyland Lions entered the fleet during the late 1920s and early '30s, the model becoming the standard single-decker. This view of a private-hire working in Kettering includes 22 of them, with Short-bodied L16 (RP 5203) bringing up the rear. *Alan Parfitt collection*

A Leyland Lion PLSC3, unfortunately unidentified, outside its Lancashire birthplace when brand-new in 1929. Its 35-seat bodywork is probably also of Leyland manufacture, although similar bodies were built by Short, under sub-contract.
Mike Sutcliffe collection

two months later came a more significant purchase, that of the Northampton Motor Omnibus Co Ltd. The routes, based on Northampton, allowed United Counties to expand into new areas, including north to Market Harborough and south into Buckinghamshire to Stony Stratford. Five Daimler Y-type single-deckers from the NMOC fleet were included in the deal but were soon sold, and to operate the new services a batch of 25 Leyland Lion saloons was ordered and delivered during the summer. A third takeover in 1928 was of York, Irchester, who worked a service into Wellingborough using a little Thornycroft A1. Several small operators were acquired in 1929, although only one of these purchases, Crick & Compton of Desborough, included a vehicle, in this case a Reo.

New buses in 1930 were Leyland Lion LT1s and Titan TD1s, the latter including a former demonstrator. A further Lion, albeit an earlier PLSC3 model, came with the business of Bagshaw, Kettering, in January 1930. The other takeover in 1930 was that of two routes and four vehicles (three Tilling-Stevens and a Maudslay) of Clarke Bros, Weedon.

The year 1931 was a notable one for the bus industry as a whole as the Road Traffic Act 1930 came into effect. The purpose of the Act was to bring some degree of order to bus and coach operation; the previous system had been pretty chaotic, whereas the new Act required services to be licensed and vehicles to be maintained to a set standard. This was overseen by the newly introduced Traffic Commissioners, organised into 13 Traffic

B15 (BD 209), the reconstructed Leyland 'Charabus', looking resplendent *en route* to Showbus '89, passing Woburn church with owner Mike Sutcliffe at the wheel. *Author*

Ma 7368
UP WELLINGBORO' 10ᵈ

NORTHAMPTON

ROTHWELL

KETTERING

RUSHDEN

RAUNDS

Areas, to whom all services had to be justified. This cut out wasteful competition but inevitably led to many smaller operators' selling out to their larger competitors. However, this stability allowed the surviving operators to invest more confidently and to consolidate and expand, which is exactly what United Counties was able to do.

Seven further operators were acquired in 1931, gradually adding more of Northamptonshire to the company's territory. Expansion also took place eastwards, where Huntingdonshire was reached by the purchase of the market-day service from Rushden of H. J. Newman; vehicles taken into stock included Reo, GMC and Chevrolet types. Buses bought new were more Leyland Titan TD1s, allowing the withdrawal of earlier Leylands, ex-Wellingborough stock and non-standard acquired types.

The early years of the United Counties story can be conveniently brought to a conclusion with the entry onto the scene of Thomas Tilling Ltd, which bought a controlling interest in the company in 1931.

2. Expansion, War and Peace

United Counties further consolidated its position in Northamptonshire in 1932, which turned out to be a bumper year for takeovers — 10 in all. Only three of the 10 involved the purchase of vehicles — White of Brixworth, with a Bedford WLG and a Dennis G, Abram of Earls Barton, with a trio of Thornycrofts and a Commer Invader, and Phillips of Long Buckby, whose fleet included a Star, a Chevrolet, an ADC and a pair of Reo 20-seaters. Also of note amongst the rest were the services between Northampton and Wolverton operated jointly by G. E. Richardson and W. A. Nightingale & Sons.

Considerable expansion by the company, often well away from its existing territory, continued in 1933. The seven acquisitions made between January and July were concerned mainly with further consolidation around Northampton, Wellingborough and Kettering, although the Stamford Motor Bus Co allowed the company to expand northeastwards. However, the rolling stock inherited was apparently less than welcome, the Chevrolet, Lancia, Reo, Dennis and Federal being soon disposed of. A similar mixed bag came with the services of Bagshawe, Kettering — a Gilford, a Chevrolet, two Reos and two Thornycrofts. Working for small companies, these little buses had been ideal for the tasks required of them, but the standardisation desired by United Counties would soon see them replaced.

On 20 September 1933 the name of the company was altered to its present title — the United Counties Omnibus Company Limited. The livery was also changed, green and cream replacing the previous blue and red. By this time the fleet total stood at 154; all double-deckers were Leyland Titans, either TD1 or TD2s, whilst the single-deckers were mainly Leyland Lions, together with a handful of acquired saloons.

December 1933 saw interesting developments on the southern borders of United Counties' operating area. The Aylesbury Omnibus Co Ltd had been taken over in 1931 by Premier Line of Shepherd's Bush, London; in May 1933, following the absorption of its parent company, Premier Omnibus, into the London Passenger Transport Board, it passed to fellow Tilling company Eastern National, which was required to break up the company and distribute its routes amongst neighbouring operators. Thus, with effect from 1 December 1933,

The entire new bus intake for 1932 was made up of 16 all-Leyland Titan TD2s, the last of which numerically was TN34 (NV 1258). As 257, and looking in fine fettle, the TD2 stands in Sheep Street, Wellingborough, on 4 April 1950, with a modest load bound for Isham, around four miles to the north. Despite its apparent good condition, the bus would be withdrawn at the end of the year. *D. C. Fisk / Alan Cross collection*

Leyland Titan TD2 TN35 (NV 2268) shows off its Eastern Counties body in this official view from 1933, which illustrates the elaborate original blue and red livery style soon to be replaced by Tilling's green. A new ECW body would be fitted in 1949, prolonging its life until 1956. *Maurice Doggett collection*

Of the fleet acquired with the Allchin business in December 1933, the only vehicles to survive for any length of time were three Leyland Tiger TS3s and three AEC Regals, all six ultimately being rebodied. With its 1937 Mumford body, 318 (VV 693) stands at Oxford's Gloucester Green bus station, probably not long before withdrawal in December 1950. *Alan Parfitt collection*

United Counties received five rural routes from Aylesbury, Fenny Stratford and Leighton Buzzard. At the same time the Stony Stratford garage, together with 10 routes, was taken over from Eastern National. The transfers included 11 vehicles — two ADCs, two Leyland Lions, three Leyland Titan TD1 double-deckers and four Leyland Tiger TS3s.

Clearly 1 December 1933 was a significant date in the company's history, for on the same day United Counties concluded a deal which brought a wealth of long-distance coach services. The business of Allchin & Son, Northampton, had included the building of steam road locomotives and road haulage, whilst the carriage of passengers in the 1920s had seen a rapid expansion into coaching. As a result United Counties gained services well away from its traditional area of operation in Northamptonshire and north Buckinghamshire, the takeover bringing routes from

Nottingham and Northampton to London and from Northampton to Birmingham, to Peterborough, and to Derby, as well as seaside journeys linking Nottingham with Hastings, Bournemouth with Lowestoft and Northampton with Skegness and Torquay. Tours and excursions were also undertaken from Northampton, Torquay, Coventry and London. The 31 vehicles involved were mainly Daimler CF6s but included a few AEC Regals, Leyland Tiger TS3s, Reos and a couple of Brockways. Most of the fleet was withdrawn by 1936, although the Leylands and AECs were rebodied and would survive into the 1950s.

The expansion continued apace during 1934. The first takeover of the year, on 29 January, was that of W. C. Nutt, who traded as Bluebell Motor Service; this brought a couple of routes to the west of Northampton, but no vehicles were acquired. February was a bumper month for the purchase of operators, with seven joining the fold. On the 5th, W. A. Nightingale of Northampton and S. C. Kingston sold their joint services in the Northampton/ Towcester area, together with quite a collection of vehicles composed of Maudslay, Gilford, Studebaker, Brockway, GMC, Guy and Reo types. On the 19th came a trio of Buckingham operators — Joseph Dunkley, Lewis Tibbetts and A. J. & A. G. Varney, bringing a number of routes but only two

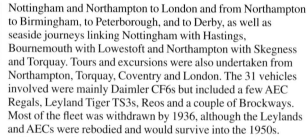

Regals were all subsequently rebodied, running thus until 1950; the Varsity name too was retained, surviving until after the war.

Further inroads were made in the Stony Stratford area with the acquisition on 8 October 1934 of R. W. Humphrey, of Old Stratford. The three buses taken into stock comprised a Chevrolet and two Leylands — a Lioness and a Cub — the latter pair each putting in around 10 years' work with their new owner. The takeover on 28 October of Frost's Motors (Kettering) Ltd brought a whole raft of services in the area as well as four seaside services to the East Coast, together with a mixed bag of vehicles, including four Leyland PLSC1 Lions that had originated with Hants & Dorset Motor Services. Finally for 1934, on 28 October, United Counties bought out W. M. Rice, acquiring one bus — a Bedford WLB, 400 (NV 5108) — and one route, between Woolaston and Wellingborough. It should be noted that in July 1934, in the midst of all the expansion, the company had moved its Head Office from Irthlingborough to Northampton. All in all quite a year!

By the early 1930s, in order to protect themselves against an advertising campaign being waged by the railway companies, coach operators in some areas were beginning to co-ordinate their services. The best-known instance was probably Associated Motorways, a pool of operators formed on 1 July 1934. The initial members were Black & White Motorways, Red & White Services, Elliott Bros ('Royal Blue'), Greyhound Motor Services, the Birmingham & Midland Motor Omnibus Co ('Midland Red') and United Counties. Each would be allotted a percentage of mileage to be run and revenue received based on 1933 figures. For United Counties in each case this amounted to a little over 3% — the lowest of the constituents. Two services were placed in the pool — Northampton–Torquay and Northampton–Bournemouth/Southsea.

buses, although the network of services running south from Northampton into Buckinghamshire was now considerable. On the 26th the business of M. E. Jelley (Jelley's Coachways) of Cosgrove was acquired; as well as local services in the Stony Stratford, Stewkley and Leighton Buzzard areas, Jelley's ran a coach service from Cosgrove to London (Central London Coach Station) using a Grose-bodied Crossley (NV 728) which became United Counties 368 and would not be withdrawn until 1938. On the same day the variety of operators in the area was further reduced with the sale of the business of J. E. Bates, Wolverton, to United Counties via Eastern National; included in the deal were a Star, a Reo and a Chevrolet, and amongst the routes was a workmen's service from Stantonbury to Cowley, near Oxford.

United Counties gained a rather more substantial presence in Oxford from 22 April 1934, when the service to London, formerly operated by the Varsity Express Motors Ltd, was transferred from Eastern Counties, which company had taken over Varsity in August 1933. The deal included tour and excursion licences from Oxford, six AEC Regals (which became UCOC 374-9) and a garage and booking office in Oxford. The

On the vehicle front, only five new buses entered the fleet during 1934 (contrasting with the 50 that came with the various takeovers). Tilling-Stevens B39A7s fitted with 32-seat Eastern Counties bodywork, they replaced a similar number of Dennis Lancets diverted to West Yorkshire Road Car. All would serve a respectable 16 years with United Counties, four being loaned to London Transport during 1940/1.

There were just two takeovers during 1935. W. F. Pack, of Brigstock, north-east of Kettering, sold out on 1 February, yielding three routes, two Bedford WLBs and a Gilford; no vehicles were involved with the takeover on 22 April of A. R. Surridge, Harpole — just a route into Northampton and a workmen's service in the town. Twelve new buses were delivered in 1935, these being five Leyland Tiger TS7s and seven Leyland Titan TD4s, all bodied by Eastern Counties.

Significantly, 1936 saw the introduction of the company's first Bristol — a chassis type that under Tilling and subsequent British Transport Commission influence was to become standard. The first examples were JO5G models, with bodywork by either Eastern Coach Works (ECW) — as successor to Eastern Counties — or Burlingham. In 1937 came no fewer than 25 further JO5Gs and the first eight of many K5G double-deckers, allowing the withdrawal of non-standard acquired rolling stock.

By 1936 the acquisition of smaller operators had slowed down. On 8 March United Counties bought out L. Timson & Son of Burton Latimer, gaining a Reo, two Gilfords and two Commer Centaurs, along with several local routes and Tours & Excursion licences from Burton Latimer and Kettering. More rural routes around Kettering (but no vehicles) were acquired on

 Kettering is the location for Bristol K5G/ECW 482 (VV 6350), representing the fleet's first Bristol double-deckers. All eight of the batch arrived at the very end of 1937 and would survive until 1955/6. In this view, 482 is working south to Rushden on 4 April 1950. *D. C. Fisk / Alan Cross collection*

27 September with the business of H. Buckby & Son, Rothwell, whilst on 24 January 1937 came that of R. L. Seamarks of Higham Ferrers, bringing with it five routes and a Tours & Excursion licence based on Rushden; also included were three Gilfords and a pair of double-deckers — an AEC Regent and a Dodson-bodied Maudslay Mentor.

In January 1936 the company experienced an 11-day strike over working conditions imposed by the Tilling regime, and there were some ugly scenes when 'blackleg' labour was brought in to try to operate some sort of service. Buses were regularly stoned and tyres deflated, and it took the intervention of the Traffic Commissioners to bring the two sides

Northampton's new bus and coach station opened in Derngate in 1936. This substantial, very Tilling-looking building is pictured *c*1950, with ex-Plymouth Corporation (via Western National) Leyland TD1 636 (DR 9066) lurking within. *Michael Rooum*

17

The first Bristol L5Gs for United Counties were 19 with Eastern Coach Works bodywork, delivered at the end of 1938 and numbered 485-503. This wartime view of 501 (ANV 421) outside the 'Lord Nelson' at Bozeat, in the company of driver J. H. Edmunds and conductor Len Robinson, shows the vehicle to be in excellent condition externally, despite the prevailing hostilities. Renumbered 247 in March 1952, it would eventually be withdrawn in August 1957, being amongst the last of the batch to go. *D. Edmunds / Roger Warwick collection*

A postwar picture of another of the 1938 Bristol L5Gs, this time pressed into express service. Probably engaged on Associated Motorways duties, 490 (VV 7255) is seen here loading at Cheltenham *c*1950. The sight of the driver tying down luggage on the roof would be too much for today's Health & Safety officer! *M. Mogridge*

together. More positively, a new bus and coach station was finally opened at Derngate, Northampton, in March 1936 (having been brought into use progressively since 1934), while 1937 saw the completion of a major extension to the works in Houghton Road, Northampton. New garages, designed in an attractive Tilling style, were also opened during this period, at Kettering (1935), Rushden and Wellingborough (both in 1938).

The final prewar takeovers were the six acquisitions made during 1938. Several services in the Stony Stratford area came on 1 May with the businesses of C. Eglesfield (Creamline Tours) and a Mrs J. Brown. Included was a workmen's service to Luton (Vauxhall) from Stony Stratford. None of the four buses inherited — two Bedfords, a Star and a Chevrolet — lasted long with their new owner. Both S. Smith of Irthlingborough (on 3 May) and W. Oakley of Wellingborough (on 22 June) sold their Tours & Excursion licences to United Counties, the former contributing a Grose-bodied Leyland Cub also. On 26 June F. Abbott relinquished his Great Doddington–Wellingborough service, but no vehicle was involved. The last independent of any size left in Northamptonshire to provide a stage-carriage service, Frank and Elizabeth Beeden, trading as Green Bus Service, also

succumbed on 26 June; included in the deal were four services and 18 vehicles, although the mixed fleet, consisting of Tilling-Stevens, Lancia, Gilford and AEC types, was soon disposed of. Finally, J. Meadows of Barton Seagrave sold out on 4 December, his services, based on Kettering, and fleet — a mixed bag of Bedford, Dennis, Leyland and GMC types — all passing initially to United Counties, although in July 1939 sections of route out towards Thrapston and Huntingdon would pass to Eastern National, along with five of the vehicles.

New deliveries in 1938 consisted of 19 Bristol L5Gs with ECW bodywork, the first examples of a combination set to be the standard saloon until the appearance of the LS in 1952. New coaches materialised as a quartet of Burlingham-bodied Leyland Tiger TS8s, 506-9 (VV 7280-3), which would spend much of their lives on the Oxford–London run.

The first new buses to be delivered in 1939 were a pair of little Dennis Ace saloons with 20-seat Mumford bodywork, for use on rural routes from Northampton and Kettering; there was, of course, nothing in the Bristol range with this sort of seating capacity. Other buses to record were four Bristol KG5s and a dozen L5Gs, all with ECW bodywork.

Wartime deliveries, as might be expected, were few and far between, although the 12 L5Gs recorded above were actually received in November and December 1939. Normal deliveries were also possible in 1940, in which year 17 L5Gs and five K5Gs were taken into stock, the double-deckers, 667-71 (BBD 811-5), being unusual in having Roe bodywork. But between these and the 1948 intake only seven new buses entered the United Counties fleet: in 1942 came a pair of Bristol K5Gs with Duple utility bodies, 614/5 (BRP 232/3), and two Brush-bodied Guy Arabs, 617/8 (BRP 787/8), while a trio of Bristol K6As, with bodywork by Strachans, were taken into stock as 630-2 (CBD 762-4) in November 1944.

Although new buses were thin on the ground during the war, a number were rebodied, whilst others had their capacities increased. The latter included some single-deckers fitted with perimeter seating, allowing an increase in standing passengers.

In common with many operators during the war, United Counties was the recipient of a number of second-hand buses, mostly double-deckers, together with a number of vehicles received on hire. In order to cover for buses under overhaul, during 1941 some 13 double-deckers were hired from Tilling subsidiary Brighton, Hove & District, these comprising Dennis Lance, Bristol GO5G and AEC Regent types. Three further AEC Regents were received on loan in 1943 in the shape of London Transport ST511/25, 621, which returned to the capital during the following year. In the other direction, four Tilling-Stevens saloons of 1934 were loaned to London Transport between October 1940 and February 1941. Contributing to a total of 473 buses (and trolleybuses) loaned to the LPTB during this period, they were allocated initially to the Central Area; however, from 30 November 1940 all single-deckers were dispersed to the Country Area, the Tilling-Stevens thereafter operating reasonably close to home, from Luton (LS) garage.

Acquired buses taken into stock during 1943 were six 1931/2-vintage AEC Regents, also from Brighton, Hove & District; having had their open-staircase bodies (by either Dodson or Tilling) scrapped, five of these were fitted with new ECW products, the sixth being broken up and used as a source of spares. During the closing stages of the war, in March 1945, six Leyland Titan double-deckers (one TD2, the rest TD1s) were bought from Western National; originating with Plymouth Corporation, these too were rebodied before entering service, their Leyland bodies being replaced by Beadle or (in the case of the TD2) Willowbrook. Finally, also in 1945, a pair of 1929 Leyland Lions were bought for spares from West Yorkshire Road Car.

For United Counties, as for other operators, the war brought fuel rationing, cuts in services, staff shortages and so on. For the year ending November 1940 the company was responsible for the dispersal of 38,000 children evacuated to destinations throughout Northamptonshire, deemed to be a 'safe' county. Five Leyland Lions were converted into ambulances for the

The first proper wartime deliveries were five Bristol K5Gs bodied by Roe, presumably because ECW was unable to fulfil the order. New in May 1940, they would retain their original bodies until withdrawal in 1958. No 667 (BBD 811) is pictured in Northampton in the 1950s. *Alan Parfitt collection*

The few wartime deliveries included three Strachans-bodied Bristol K6As, in 1944. Having already had their AEC engines replaced by Gardner units, all would receive new Bristol bodies in 1954, running thereafter for a further 10 years. Looking suitably austere with its original body, 708 (CBD 763) is seen between Wellingborough and Irchester in 1952 or 1953. *Alan Parfitt collection*

Amongst the hired buses from Brighton, Hove & District during the war was 6332 (ANJ 832), which United Counties numbered H8. It was one of three Bristol GO5Gs with open-top Tilling bodies which were subsequently fitted with roofs by ECW. Following a four-year stint with United Counties it would return to the South Coast in November 1945, working until withdrawal and sale to Crosville in 1951.
Ian Allan Library

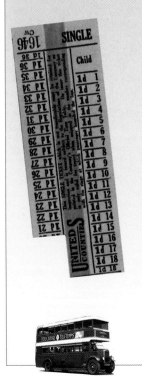

Ministry of Health in 1939 and eventually disappeared overseas, whilst six further Leyland Lions were requisitioned in August 1941. With regards to enemy action, Northamptonshire escaped relatively lightly, despite the presence of significant industry in Wellingborough, Kettering and Northampton. Although a few bombs did fall on Northampton itself, the most damage appears to have been caused by a crippled RAF Stirling that crashed on the town centre in July 1941. Despite considerable destruction, the only fatality was the pilot.

In May 1940 Irthlingborough garage became the home of Eastern Coach Works (initially on lease but later sold); the latter's Lowestoft factory was deemed to be in an area vulnerable to invasion and was given 24 hours' notice to cease production. One by-product of the move was the need to open a small garage elsewhere in Irthlingborough to house the two single-deckers allocated there. Eastern Coach Works would eventually return to Lowestoft in 1945, although limited production would continue at Irthlingborough until July 1952.

From the beginning of 1942, in a complicated deal, United Counties, jointly with City of Oxford Motor Services and Eastern National, took responsibility for an Oxford–Bedford service previously operated by Blue Coach Services of Bedford. Eastern National took over United Counties' share later in the year, although this would revert to United Counties in May 1952, as will be described later.

In an effort to save fuel, the Government urged operators of any size to run buses on gas, usually in the form of a trailer in which anthracite was burned to produce the required gas. Despite high hopes, only 17 members of the United Counties fleet were so modified — rather fewer than the 26 (or 10%) stipulated by the Government. The vehicles involved were Leyland Titan TD1s 191/9, 203-5/7, Leyland Tiger TS7s 312-5, 401-5, Leyland Lion PLSC3 110 and Bristol JO5G 459. They ran mainly from Wellingborough garage but also from Kettering. Overall, the gas buses were not popular; they were slow, making good time-keeping difficult, the fumes were said to be unpleasant for both crews and passengers, and the towing of the trailers caused instability. They were not missed when, following the Allied invasion of Europe, the supply of oil improved, allowing the abandonment of the scheme. With the exception of 110 all gas buses were converted back to petrol or diesel in 1944/5.

Even following the end of hostilities production was still severely restricted, and 1946, the first full year of peace, saw no new buses join the United Counties fleet. In consequence more

Leyland Lions were rebodied, while eight 1936-vintage Bristol JO5Gs were refurbished, swapping bodies at the same time. The following year, 1947, brought forth no fewer than three new buses, a trio of Bristol K5Gs with ECW bodywork arriving as 639-41 (DBD 980-2).

During 1946 the bus-operating industry was getting itself back to some sort of order, including the resumption of coach services, which were generally amongst the most disrupted, having ceased altogether in 1942. As far as United Counties was concerned, the Oxford–London route was re-started from 25 February, whilst that from Nottingham to London had to wait until 6 July. A Tours & Excursion programme was also possible in 1946, prewar licensing procedures, suspended and subsequently succeeded by wartime emergency powers, being relaxed from 1 July. Although the situation with regard to staffing levels and vehicle maintenance was improving only gradually, it is interesting to note that, outside London, almost double the number of passengers (over 8 million in 1946, as opposed to over 4 million in 1938) were now being transported, and this with a largely worn-out bus fleet and a severe staff shortage.

Also hired from Brighton, Hove & District during the last war were four Tilling-bodied AEC Regents, which, like the Bristol GO5Gs, were open-top when they arrived and were fitted with detachable roofs by ECW. Three ran for United Counties between September 1941 and 1945, the exception being H12 (GJ 2008), seen here in Daventry, which returned south in August 1943. This bus would be another to pass to Crosville on withdrawal, in 1949.
A. W. Mace collection / The Omnibus Society

March 1945 saw the arrival of five Leyland TD1s and a solitary TD2 from Plymouth Corporation (via Western National); TD1 510 (DR 9066), carrying the Beadle body that replaced its Leyland original, is seen on a works service in Northampton *c*1953. *Roy Marshall*

The Government of the time (Labour since July 1945) was embarking on a programme of nationalisation of key industries — coal, iron and steel, gas and electricity and transport. The Transport Act, passed on 6 August 1947, became effective from 1 January 1948 with the creation of the British Transport Commission. This immediately affected the railways and road haulage but not the buses. The Tilling group, pre-empting any possible compulsory purchase, sold out to the state in the September, in a deal backdated to 1 January, the United Counties fleet being part of a total of 8,000-plus buses and coaches (together with the chassis-manufacturing plant at Bristol and Eastern Coach Works at Lowestoft) thus passing to Government control.

Many of the 1928/9 intake of Leyland PLSC3 Lions received new Willowbrook bodies (and Bristol radiators) in 1945/6, extending their lives for a few more years. Withdrawn in 1952, 164 (RP 6805) is seen some four years later, languishing as a non-PSV at Calverley Quarries. It appears to be in the condition in which it left United Counties and still displays a blind for a short working on route 46 (Northampton–Buckingham–Aylesbury).
Maurice Doggett collection

Among the first buses to be delivered to United Counties in 1948 were six Bedford OBs with Beadle bodies, 101-6 (DBD 936-41), ordered back in 1946. Also delivered during the course of the year were eight more Bristol K5Gs, although four of these were immediately loaned to London Transport, now also nationalised and under the control of the British Transport Commission; being of lowbridge type, with a side gangway upstairs, they must have caused interest to some passengers in the capital! Also received in 1948 were two Bristol L6Bs to dual-purpose specification. The same year saw the building of small garages at Corby and Daventry, whilst the purchase of a shed for one bus was effected at Market Harborough during the following year.

Sixteen further Bristol K5Gs/K6Bs arrived in 1949, although four of these joined the aforementioned quartet in service in London. More surprising was the appearance of a couple of Beadle-Morris saloons (Morris Commercial running units built within a Beadle frame and body — an uncommon combination) diverted from Brighton, Hove & District; the pair would be the last non-Bristol vehicles bought new by United Counties for more than 30 years, until the first Leyland Nationals entered service at the beginning of 1973. In the late 1940s further Bristol JO5Gs and Leyland Titans were having a bit more life squeezed out of them through being fitted with new ECW bodywork.

3. Uniting More Counties

The new decade began in the same fashion as the old one had ended, with the continuing replacement of prewar rolling stock. Deliveries for 1950 amounted to some 41 new vehicles, all to the familiar Bristol/ECW combination. Double-deckers were the last K5Gs and K6Bs, followed by the first KS5Gs and KS6Bs. Although the Bristol K had been the biggest-selling variant (2,796 in prewar and postwar forms), the longer KS sold only 231 during its short production run, just 14 running with United Counties from new. Single-decker buses joining the fleet in 1950 comprised four Bristol L5Gs (three of which were a diverted order from Caledonian Omnibus) and eight of the longer LL5G (5) and LL6B (3). Rather more exotic were half a dozen Bristol L6B coaches which arrived in time for the summer season. Withdrawals included Leyland Lions, TD1s and TD2s, the five 1934 Tilling-Stevens and a number of coaches that had originated with Allchin, Eastern Counties and Eastern National.

In 1951 United Counties took delivery of its last four Bristol KS variants and its first examples of the 8ft-wide KSW, Bristol's replacement for the KS. (The four KS types also carried the wider body, demonstrating a noticeable overhang from certain angles.) The new legislation allowing 8ft-wide buses saw the Bristol LWL6B enter the fleet, 14 arriving during the year. Further coaches were 13 Bristol LL6B carrying 8ft-wide full-fronted ECW bodywork to the 'Queen Mary' design. They were quite luxurious and, being longer, seated 37 rather than the 31 of

Further coaches were delivered to United Counties in 1951 in the shape of 13 Bristol LL6Bs with so-called 'Queen Mary' ECW bodywork, seating 37. Seen loading for London in Nottingham during the mid-1950s is 375 (FRP 840). *John Aldridge collection*

the L6Bs. The year also saw prewar Bristol JO5G chassis going to Lowestoft to receive new ECW bodies.

A decision was also made in 1951 that would have a far-reaching effect on the company's fortunes. The British Transport Commission was keen to 'tidy up' certain areas of its bus operations, and an agreement was reached in December to transfer Eastern National's Midland Area to United Counties. With Eastern National's headquarters being situated in Chelmsford, Essex, that company's Midland Area, covering Huntingdonshire, Bedfordshire, north Buckinghamshire and north Hertfordshire, was very much out on a limb operationally. Aylesbury was indeed a long way from the Essex coast! Furthermore, it was of a similar size to United Counties, and it made sense to combine the two into a fleet of around 550 vehicles, the considered ideal size for a Tilling fleet being around 500. (It wasn't all bad news for Eastern National, however, for it subsequently took control of and later absorbed Westcliff-on-Sea Motor Services, which included a service to London.)

The enlarged United Counties commenced operation on 1 May 1952. Some 247 buses and coaches were transferred (all but eight being operational), along with over a hundred routes throughout the aforementioned area and nine summer-only express services to seaside destinations. United Counties also superseded Eastern National in the co-ordination agreement with Luton Corporation Transport Department, under which routes in Luton and Dunstable were run as 'Luton & District Transport'. Property inherited included depots at Aylesbury, Bedford, Biggleswade, Hitchin, Huntingdon, Luton and Stony Stratford, with outstations at Cambridge, Clophill, St Neots and Yardley Hastings (of Bedford) and Dunstable, Leighton Buzzard and Toddington (of Luton). There were also various other premises, together with the small 1939-built bus station at St Peter's, Bedford.

Now pitched together as one, the two areas were designated as Western and Eastern and remained operationally separate, a situation that pertained well into the 1960s. The Eastern area

One of the smaller garages to be taken over from Eastern National was that in Gas Street, Toddington, north of Luton. Opened in 1923 by Road Motors Ltd, which was taken over by National Omnibus in 1925, it lasted through Eastern National and United Counties ownership, eventually being closed by Luton & District in October 1988, when a new depot was opened in Dunstable. Pictured in August 1987, the building is now a house. *Author*

If Toddington was one of the smallest garages to be taken over from Eastern National, that in North Street, Leighton Buzzard, may have been the most decrepit. In Eastern National and early United Counties days it was rented on a part-time basis; rather in the manner of a cheap seaside boarding house, buses were unable to gain access between 8am and 6pm. Sold to Bedfordshire County Council in 1973, it was formally leased to United Counties in 1981. Despite threats of demolition, it survived to pass to Luton & District in 1986 and was even repainted before being replaced by a new facility in the town in August 1988; the cramped little site now contains housing. This view shows ex-Luton Corporation Bristol RELL6L 385 (UXD 125G) standing outside the garage in April 1979. *Author*

was the more urban in character; indeed, Luton was the company's most profitable town. However, with the Head Office being at Northampton, it was a long-standing complaint that the best vehicles were allocated to the Western Area. It also became increasingly clear that the five-cylinder buses at Luton were less than suited to the hilly nature of the town and to the increasingly difficult traffic conditions, and the early 1960s would see Bristol K6Bs transferred from the Western Area to alleviate this problem.

Staff turnover in Luton was high due to the presence in the town of other major employers, such as Vauxhall Motors and SKF. Furthermore, an agreement was in place preventing the poaching of staff from Luton Corporation (and *vice versa*).

The buses and coaches that were taken into stock were an interesting collection, with the emphasis on the Bristol/ECW combination, as might be

expected from a former Tilling company. The most numerous type was the Bristol K5G, totalling 89 vehicles, ranging from the FPU-registered batch of 1937 to the ONO batch of 1949/50; many of the older chassis had been rebodied, while others would follow suit after transfer. In May 1952 all garages had an allocation of the type, the greatest concentration (28) being at Bedford. The last of these K5Gs would be retired from passenger service in 1967; in the meantime (from 1961) several of the wartime JEV batch would see further service with neighbouring Luton Corporation. The remaining Bristol double-deckers acquired from Eastern National were five KS5Gs of 1950 and nine KSW5Gs new in 1951, all of the latter surviving into National Bus Company ownership.

The Leyland Titan in its various forms constituted the remaining double-deckers to come with Eastern National, 42 in total. The three TD1s were soon disposed of, whilst of four TD2s only a pair Weymann-bodied examples new to Plymouth Corporation did any work for their new owners. Four of the five 1935 TD3s still carried their original Eastern Counties bodies and were soon withdrawn, the remaining machine, 546 (BTW 498), surviving at Luton until 1956 by virtue of its 1949 ECW body. The 10 TD4s dating from 1936/7 were also soon laid aside, although two that had been rebodied in 1949/50 would work until 1956. The other prewar Leyland 'deckers were eight 1937-built TD5s, all of which had been rebodied by ECW in 1949/50; these, like the TD4s, were shared between Luton and

29

The bulk of the double-deckers that came from Eastern National were prewar-specification Bristol K5Gs. Still with its original ECW body of 1940, 674 (JEV 413) is pictured at Park Square, Luton, on working to Hitchin shortly before withdrawal in 1956. *Bristol Vintage Bus Group*

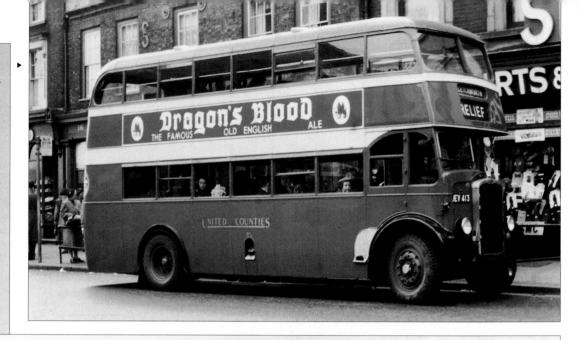

Bristol K5G 693 (JEV 432) on the other hand, received a new ECW body, in 1953. The effect of fitting an 8ft-wide body onto a 7ft 6in chassis is evident in this view of 693 at Huntingdon in June 1958. *Essex Bus Enthusiasts' Group*

The most modern of the Bristols acquired from Eastern National were the nine KSW5Gs, all less than a year old. Apparently in ex-works condition, 876 (SHK 519) is seen heading out from Northampton towards Towcester in the mid-1960s; at this time it was allocated to Biggleswade so was probably being 'run in'. The whole batch would survive into NBC ownership, 876 not being withdrawn until March 1970.
Chris Lodington

The Leyland TD5s inherited from Eastern National lasted until 1956/7; 575 (FEV 181), with 1950 ECW body, looks in good shape on service 52 from Luton to Hitchin and Letchworth.
Three Counties Bus & Commercial Vehicle Museum collection

Inherited from Eastern National in May 1952 were 10 Leyland TD4s were, eight at Luton and two at Hitchin. Seen in Station Road, Luton, on local route 57 from Leagrave, Brush-bodied 561 (DEV 488) of 1936 was photographed on 19 July 1952 from the footbridge that linked Midland and Bute Street stations.
J. F. Bearman

The impressive looking ECW-bodied Leyland PD1s
were shared between Luton and Bedford garages.
Two of the latter's allocation, 585/92 (MPU 38, 46),
flank Bristol K5G 716 (KNO 598) in 1956.
Author's collection

The 15 prewar Bristol L5Gs
all carried GPU registrations;
253 (GPU 420) touts for
business in Silver Street,
Bedford, c1953.
*Robert Mack / Alan Parfitt
collection*

Hitchin garages, but would work until 1956/7. Finally, and very much the pick of the crop, were a dozen youthful (1947/8) Leyland PD1As with ECW bodies, evenly divided between Luton and Bedford garages. Latterly concentrated at Bedford, these popular buses would remain with the company until 1959, all then passing to Cumberland Motor Services. (Of interest is that, before their departure, they were repainted red and fitted with 'T'-style destination displays; in which condition the last examples would survive with Cumberland until 1965.)

Of the former Eastern National single-deckers, the majority were, again, of the Bristol/ECW combination. The earliest were the 20 JO5G models, five being Eastern Counties-bodied coaches of 1936, of which United Counties took little time in disposing; the other 15 were all ECW-bodied buses, and these too generally had short lives with their new owners, the one

exception, 194 (ENO 960), receiving a Willowbrook body from Leyland Lion 159 (RP 6722), with which it soldiered on until 1956. The Bristol L5G, contemporary of the K5G, accounted for 35 vehicles, three of which were classified as dual-purpose. Dating from between 1938 and 1950, they were well spread around the area (although nearly half were at Bedford on takeover) and would survive until 1964. The L5G's successors, the LL5G and LWL5G, were also represented, numbering 13 examples between them, and would last until the late 1960s. The remaining Bristols were a trio of L6B coaches, 352-4 (PTW 107-9), which worked for a few seasons before returning to Eastern National in 1958.

The other single-deck vehicles taken over were a rag-bag of Dennis Lancets, small Bedfords, Leylands and a Tilling-Stevens, most of which were almost immediately withdrawn and sold.

One of nine Bristol LL5G saloons inherited from Eastern National, 384 (RHK 122) is seen arriving in Aylesbury from Stony Stratford in November 1962. *Philip Wallis*

The three Bristol L6B/ECW coaches were impressive machines but were destined to become outdated with the arrival of the Bristol LS and would be returned to Eastern National in 1958. Bedford-allocated 353 (PTW 108) is pictured in the London suburbs, possibly on a private-hire working. *Roy Marshall collection*

Seen here as Eastern National 3555, Dennis
Lancet I BTW 494 was numbered 106 by
United Counties but would survive as such
for only a month. *Alan Parfitt collection*

The longest-lasting (both at Aylesbury, having originated with Queen's Park Coaches) were two of the coaches, Yeates-bodied Dennis Lancet III 160 (MPP 450) and Leyland Tiger PS1/Duple 170 (KKX 408) remaining in the United Counties fleet until 1956 and 1957 respectively.

The virtual doubling of the fleet required a vehicle-renumbering programme, existing United Counties stock being dealt with on 1 March 1952, to be followed by the Eastern National vehicles upon acquisition two months later. Single-deckers were allocated numbers between 100 and 499, double-deckers being numbered between 500 and 999. Number plates were affixed to the vehicles, following Eastern National practice, replacing the painted-on numbers previously used by United Counties. To denote allocation, each plate was colour-coded, as follows:

Aylesbury — light blue with red edges
Bedford — light blue
Biggleswade — light blue with black edges
Hitchin — brown with black edges
Huntingdon — light blue with yellow edges
Kettering — yellow
Luton — brown
Northampton — green
Rushden — red with black edges
Stony Stratford — green with black edges
Wellingborough — red

Corby was later allocated yellow with black edges, and Stamford yellow with red edges.

The United Counties 'empire', as far as stage-carriage operations were concerned, now stretched from Leicester and Stamford in the north to Cambridge in the east, Oxford in the west and Amersham in the south; the last was reached from Aylesbury by the 359 — a joint operation with London Transport that had begun during the war and would expire in 1964. Although much of the network was rural in nature, the company's profitability was through

The longest-lived of the non-standard coaches inherited was 170 (KKX 408), the Leyland Tiger PS1/Duple that had been originally new to Queen's Park Coaches, Aylesbury, in 1947. Seen alongside Bedford depot in September 1956 in the company of one of the PD1s, it would be used by United Counties until 1957 and then re-sold to Eastern National.
J. S. Cockshott

Three of the Dennis Lancets had also originated with Queen's Park Coaches, although in fact 160 (MPP 450), a Yeates-bodied Lancet III new in 1949, was the only coach. Seen here in September 1953 at Southsea, it would survive as late as 1956.
Maurice Doggett collection

Also at Southsea on the same occasion was Bedford OB/Duple 118 (ONO 85). Assuming the date to be accurate, this would have been one of its last outings with United Counties, as it would be withdrawn during the same month.
Maurice Doggett collection

Although most of the Bedford OBs were sold, Beadle-bodied bus 113 (LPU 622) became a stores lorry in 1954, replacing Bedford WTL CEV 394 at Luton. It would fulfil this role until 1965, being seen between duties at Bedford not long before withdrawal. *Ray Crane*

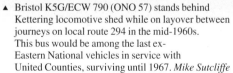

▲ Bristol K5G/ECW 790 (ONO 57) stands behind
Kettering locomotive shed while on layover between
journeys on local route 294 in the mid-1960s.
This bus would be among the last ex-
Eastern National vehicles in service with
United Counties, surviving until 1967. *Mike Sutcliffe*

A mid-'60s view inside Kettering garage, revealing an oddity among
the ex-Eastern National Bristol K5Gs. New in 1947, NNO 105 was
involved in an accident in 1951 and subsequently donated its body,
along with its registration, to a new bus; the remaining chassis frame
was rebuilt using spare parts and received a new 8ft-wide ECW body,
the ensemble being registered TTW 268. As United Counties 770
it would survive until 1965. *Mike Sutcliffe* ►►

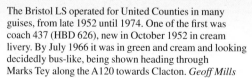

The Bristol LS operated for United Counties in many guises, from late 1952 until 1974. One of the first was coach 437 (HBD 626), new in October 1952 in cream livery. By July 1966 it was in green and cream and looking decidedly bus-like, being shown heading through Marks Tey along the A120 towards Clacton. *Geoff Mills*

urban operations in towns such as Bedford, Luton and Corby (there being at this time no town services operated by United Counties in Northampton).

The first day of May 1952 also saw the transfer from United Counties to South Midland Motor Services of the former Varsity Express Motors Oxford–London service, which was always out on a limb from the rest of the network (although it was ironic that from the same date Oxford would be served by United Counties buses on the ex-Eastern National route from Bedford). The deal included the Botley Road garage, the booking office at Gloucester Green bus station and eight Bristol/ECW coaches — L6Bs 71-4 (EBD 234-7) and LL6Bs 75-8 (FRP 832-4/6).

A final event to record for 1 May 1952 was the takeover by United Counties of the Northampton–Brixworth service which was operated by Miss Mary E. Knight of Northampton. No vehicles were acquired.

Deliveries of new vehicles to United Counties in 1952 consisted of 22 ECW-bodied Bristol KSW6Bs together with five

KSW5Gs diverted from Eastern National. Ten Bristol LWL6B saloons, four of which were to dual-purpose specification, also entered the fleet early in the year, whilst in the autumn came a new type, the Bristol LS (Light Saloon). Nos 436-8/41/2 (HNV 729, HBD 626/7/30/1) were LS5Gs, 437/8 being 39-seat coaches, the remainder 43-seat dual-door buses, and were the first underfloor-engined buses in the fleet (although a somewhat underpowered Eastern Counties demonstrator, LS4G MAH 744, the second prototype LS, had been on loan earlier in the year).

March 1953 saw a wholesale renumbering of routes in order to integrate the former Eastern National services. Briefly, these received route numbers below 250 with the old United Counties routes numbered above 250. Routes operated under the Luton & District Transport agreement remained unchanged.

The first full year of the enlarged company saw yet another takeover, set to be the last for seven years — that of long-established Bedfordshire independent O. A. Bartle & Son, of Potton. This was effective from 21 June and comprised seven

Withdrawn vehicles at Wellingborough in 1954. From left to right are former Bartle Guy Arab FMJ 752, Leyland TD4s 550/1 (NV 5138/9), ex-Eastern National Bristol JO5G 221 (FNO 791), native JO5G 203 (VV 6258), ex-Bartle Arab EBM 422, Bedford OB/Beadle 121 (DBD 938) and ex-Eastern National JO5G 223 (FNO 793); on the extreme right is Dennis Lancet 101 (AEV 785), one of the eight buses acquired from Eastern National that were not actually used by United Counties. *Ron Wellings*

Two more veterans put out to grass in 1954 were 580 (GP 6241), one of the ex-Brighton, Hove & District AEC Regents, carrying its second (ECW) body, and 512 (DR 9070), a one-time Plymouth Corporation Leyland TD1, also with its second body, in this case by Beadle; it also still carries its former fleet number, 638. *Roy Marshall collection*

stage services, two express routes and several contracts. The 15 vehicles may have looked interesting from an enthusiast's point of view, but most did no work for their new owners, even though all but a Gilford 168OT were officially allocated fleet numbers. The five Bedford OBs and four Thurgood-bodied Guy Arab III single-deck buses were withdrawn immediately, but the three Arab coaches and a pair of Arab double-deckers remained at work until September 1955, the 'deckers running from Biggleswade garage, the coaches allocated to Bedford.

More of the Bristol LS type — four more coaches and 18 dual-purpose — entered service during 1953, whilst the ranks of the Bristol KSW6B were swelled by 21 new deliveries to satisfy double-deck demands. Well, almost. Another new type was making an appearance, in the shape of 950 (JBD 955), the first of many Bristol Lodekkas. An early production model, 950 had been preceded by the loan (from West Yorkshire Road Car in 1951) of demonstrator JWT 712; allocated initially to Northampton, it would spend most of its life on town services in Luton, ultimately serving the company for more than 20 years. Also in 1953 a dozen ex-Eastern National Bristol K5Gs received new 8ft-wide bodies, allowing the wartime chassis a bit more life. Withdrawals included the 1948 Bedford OBs, as well as various elderly Leylands and prewar Bristols.

The 1954 vehicle intake included the company's first production Lodekkas, LD6Bs 951-9 (JBD 956-64), and its last KSW6Bs, 945/61-9 (JBD 982, KNV 334-42). The Lodekka had rendered the lowbridge KSW obsolete, and this final batch were amongst the last to be built (the last highbridge examples being

45

built for Brighton, Hove & District as late as 1957). Other
deliveries that year were a dozen more Bristol LS single-
deckers, including two to full coach specification. Buses leaving
the fleet included life-expired Bristol L5Gs, more Leyland
Titans and all of the ex-Brighton, Hove & District AEC Regents.
Receiving a new lease of life were two Duple-bodied Bristol
K5Gs and three Strachans-bodied Bristol K6As, their wartime
utility bodywork being replaced by products from Bristol to
ECW design; at the same time the K6As also had their AEC
engines replaced with Gardner 5LW power units.

Vehicle-wise, the 1955-7 period saw a steady flow of Bristol
Lodekka and LS types to satisfy the company's double-deck
and saloon demands. Due to a shortage of Bristol AVW
engines, a number of the Lodekkas at this time received
reconditioned six-cylinder engines taken from older saloons,
which were then re-engined as five-cylinder machines. The
only variety amongst new deliveries was provided by six

lightweight Bristol SC4LK models, which entered the fleet in
the second half of 1957. These ECW-bodied front-engined
buses seated 35 and were comparable to the Bedford SB;
indeed, Bedford supplied the axles. Numbered 125-30
(ONV 425-30), they were ordered following the loan in
January 1955 of Eastern National's prototype, 724 APU.
Nos 123-7 went to Stony Stratford, whilst 128-30 were
required at Welford (an outstation of Northampton), replacing
prewar Bristol L5Gs as the only buses to fit into the garage
(although from 1963, following modifications to their
destination boxes, three postwar L5Gs would be allocated two
at a time to Welford — as, perhaps, they should have been in
the first place!). Also notable among the 1957 deliveries were
114/5 (OBD 901/2), Bristol LS6Gs with rather luxurious
35-seat ECW coach bodies suitable for touring, a programme
of which had been initiated for the 1956 season using Bristol
LS6Bs 481/2 suitably down-seated to 35.

Bristol SC4LK/ECW 129 (ONV 429) works a 325 between
Stony Stratford and Northampton (or possibly a short working
from Wootton) *c*1960. New in 1957, this lightweight bus and
the other five of the batch would be withdrawn in 1962/3,
passing to Red & White (125-7) or Cumberland (128-30)
Roger Warwick collection

One of two Bristol LS6Gs with 35-seat ECW bodywork for tours work, 115 (OBD 902) passes through Brighton sometime during the four-year period (1957-61) that these vehicles were operated by United Counties. *Alan Parfitt collection*

Broadly similar to the touring LSs, 116/7 (OBD 903/4) seated 39 for express and private-hire duties. Photographed in the early 1960s, 117 looks good in the sunshine at Woodford Halse whilst her passengers visit the nearby locomotive shed. *Ray Crane*

In 1956 three elderly Bristol L5Gs were converted into tuition vehicles, including VV 7250, formerly bus 231, which became No 1 and served in its new role for five years.
John Aldridge collection

The early (1953-5) bus and dual-purpose Bristol LSs were originally fitted with dual doors, and from 1956 a programme was initiated to convert these to single-door. From the same year many of the coaches and all dual-purpose vehicles were repainted green with cream window surrounds — a reverse of the more pleasing cream and green used hitherto. Vehicle withdrawals during this period included the last Leyland Titan TDs, both those new to United Counties and inherited from Eastern National. Further Bristol JO5Gs and prewar L5Gs and K5Gs also bit the dust, although in 1956 three L5Gs were converted into driver-training buses, extending their lives by some five or six years. The two Beadle-Morris saloons, 168/9 (FBD 915/6) also left the fleet, in 1955, after only six years' service.

Service reductions were implemented in 1956/7 as a result of the Suez Crisis, whereby international control of the canal was threatened, and oil supplies to the UK were interrupted.

Although the situation eased from the spring of 1957 the damage was done, and many passengers found other ways to travel.

The final new Bristol LSs — dual-purpose 118-21 (PNV 218-21) — entered service in June 1958, having been in store since the previous November. All other buses to enter service in that year were Bristol LD6B Lodekkas, which banished more K5Gs from the fleet, including wartime Roe-bodied 667-71.

Service-wise, it was company policy to combine routes where practicable. One notable route created by linking existing services was an elongated 128, formed by joining the existing 128 (Northampton–Bedford) with the 149 (Bedford–Cambridge) Perhaps less successful was the marathon 141 from Aylesbury to St Ives via Leighton Buzzard and Bedford — a journey of some 70-odd miles, which took just under four hours in a lumbering LD6B. (As a child the author frequently undertook the journey between Leighton Buzzard and either

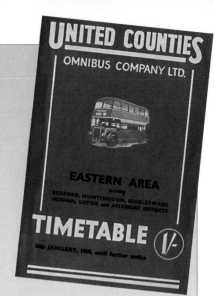

▲
Former Eastern National
Bristol K5G 681 (JEV 420)
became a tree-lopper in April
1962; this view shows the
conversion underway at
Northampton on the first
of that month. The bus would
survive in this role until 1975.
Geoff Mills

◄ A well-known recovery tender
was URP 999, an ex-Army
Foden GS truck rebuilt in 1959
and fitted with bodywork
supplied by ECW. It remained
in service until 1982 and was
subsequently preserved.
Author's collection

Aylesbury or Bedford and often wondered where this faraway place called St Ives was!)

In 1959 United Counties became the first operator to be licensed to use the newly opened initial section of the M1 motorway, albeit for duplicate workings only, on its London–Northampton–Leicester–Nottingham X1 route. The same year witnessed the appearance of another new vehicle type, the MW being Bristol's successor to the LS. Initial deliveries comprised dual-purpose 134-41 (SRP 134-36, TRP 137-41), of which the first three entered service on 1 January. Later in the year the last new Bristol LDs entered service, including 561 (TRP 561), which was the company's 100th Lodekka and carried external publicity to this effect. The Lodekkas saw off the ex-Eastern National Leyland Titan PD1s, all of which had headed north to Cumberland by the end of the year. This completed, the fleet was now all-Bristol (and would remain so until the unlikely appearance of a pair of Bedford SBs in 1967).

In 1960 the Bristol LD6B was succeeded by the FS6B, which had a flat floor (in place of the previous sunken gangway) on the lower deck. The 11 delivered that year to United Counties were 600-10 (URP 600/1, WBD 602-10), the first declaring on its advertisement panels that it was fitted with air suspension (on the rear axles). A further five Bristol MW6Gs with 41-seat dual-purpose bodywork (although classified by the company as coaches) completed the year's intake. A spot of body-swapping also took place at this time, seven 1948-vintage Bristol K5Gs gaining 1952/3-built bodies from prewar K5Gs, which in turn received the 1948 bodies and were promptly sold.

The first takeover since 1953 was that of Bedfordshire independent Keysonian Coaches of Keysoe, effective from 1 May 1960; no vehicles changed hands. On the property front, the major event of the year was the opening of a new, much-needed bus station in Bedford, to replace that built at St Peter's in 1939. Situated at Allhallows, in the centre of the town, and built as part of the area's redevelopment, it was opened by the Mayor on 1 December. In 1961 there appeared in the United Counties fleet yet another new Bristol model, the forward-entrance/exit 70-seat FLF6B; 617-22 (YNV 617-22) entered service during the second half of the year, mostly from Luton. The FLFs were preceded by six more FS6Bs, 611-6 (WBD 611-6), these featuring fluorescent interior lighting (rather than tungsten bulbs) and, in the case of 614-6, offside illuminated advertisements — a feature shared with the FLFs. For the summer season came 200-3 (YBD 200-3), MW6Gs with 34-seat ECW coach bodies, intended for tour work.

▲ *En route* from Northampton to Newport Pagnell, Bristol FLF6B/ECW 628 (YNV 628) takes on passengers at Sherington, near journey's end, on 19 October 1974. *Chris Lodington*

It was common practice for major operators to hire in coaches from independents to help out at busy periods. Here, United Counties Bristol MW6G 154 (154 BRP) loads at Northampton Derngate on an X6 journey from Nottingham to London via Luton (rather than the motorway) in 1965; the coach on hire is Bedford SB5/ Duple DNV 378C, belonging to Jeffs of Helmdon. It was a licensing condition that the operating company provide the vehicle for the main service, even if it could turn out only a bus. Although 154 was a dual-purpose vehicle, its bus livery makes the SB5 appear the more inviting vehicle!
Ray Crane

SEASIDE COACH SERVICES

UNITED COUNTIES 1961
OMNIBUS COMPANY LIMITED

On the premises front, 1961 saw a new garage brought into use at Bletchley as an outstation of Stony Stratford, replacing that at nearby Fenny Stratford with effect from January. Irthlingborough outstation closed its doors in September, operations passing to Rushden.

Vehicles entering service in 1962/3 consisted of the usual mix: FLF6Bs (18), FS6Bs (9) and dual-purpose MW6Gs (14). However, this was not quite in line with the original intention; the FS6Bs had been ordered as FSF6Bs (*i.e.* short wheelbase with forward entrance), but the FSF was discontinued, the options henceforth being either FS or FLF. Eight of the FS6Bs (641-8) received power (rather than manual) doors similar to those that would have been provided on the FSFs and (save 648, which went to Northampton) were put to work on Bedford's busiest route, the cross-town 101. Withdrawals included Bristol LS6G luxury coaches 114/5, which passed to Eastern National, as did three of the 1961 MW6G touring coaches (200-2), redundant following the sale to Wallace Arnold of the company's 13 tour licences. The six Bristol SC4LKs also left for pastures new, 125-7 passing to Red & White in 1962, 128-30 to Cumberland in 1963.

Amongst the service revisions in 1963 was the renumbering in March of routes in the Luton area, releasing numbers below 60 for possible use by Luton & District Transport Services. (A few of the new numbers survive today with Arriva the Shires, such as the 61, previously 16, linking Luton and Dunstable with Aylesbury.) In July another new bus station was opened, at Kettering; replacing various street termini, this was actually planned during the war! The year also saw the opening of another new bus station, at Stony Stratford, while depot improvements were made at this location as well as at Hitchin and Bedford.

Ex-Hants & Dorset Bristol
LL6B 433 (KEL 732) stands in
an apparently deserted
Kettering bus station in 1968
while on the Peterborough
service (or, more likely, a short
working to Thrapston).
Mike Sutcliffe

A new bus station was opened at Kettering on
7 July 1963, replacing 'on-street' termini.
Its newness is still evident on 13 August, when this
view was recorded of 936 (JBD 973), a 1953
Bristol KSW6B/ECW, loading for Thrapston
on a short working of route 266; the full journey
ran through to Peterborough and was a joint
operation with Eastern Counties. *Mike Sutcliffe*

53

This, the first temporary bus station in Luton, was in operation between August 1964 and August 1969. All buses in the picture are either United Counties Bristol Lodekkas or Luton Corporation Albion Lowlanders. Centre-stage is Bristol LD6B/ECW 979 (LNV 507), pulling away for Leighton Buzzard via Dunstable and Hockliffe. *Chris Lodington*

A second temporary bus station at Luton was in use from August 1969 until the subterranean edifice in Bute Street was opened in September 1976. This view was recorded *c*1973 and shows the Arndale shopping centre under construction in the background. This whole area in front of Luton Central Library is now pedestrianised. *Roy Dixon / Author's collection*

TIMETABLE

United Counties Omnibus Co. Ltd.
Houghton Road
Northampton
4th April 1965   1/6

It may appear strange to many that a town the size of Luton was without a bus station, and although the idea had been discussed it was not until August 1964 that a temporary bus station was opened on land situated within an area bounded by Guildford Street, Williamson Street, Library Road and Bridge Street. Used by both United Counties and Luton Corporation buses, it was to remain in use for five years, until replaced by a second temporary bus station a little further south. This period saw great upheaval with the development of the Arndale Shopping Centre over a large area of central Luton, hence the temporary

nature of these bus stations. Meanwhile, Bedford's bus station was being extended to give extra parking space and better accommodation for coach services etc, and passenger facilities at Northampton's Derngate bus station were being improved.

Express services received a boost in 1964 with the arrival of the company's first 36ft coaches, in the shape of Bristol RELH6G/ECW 250-9 (250 FRP, ABD 251- 3B, BBD 254-9B), delivered in green with cream waistbands. More mundane perhaps were another 24 Bristol FS6Bs, 650-73 (650-5 EBD, ABD 656-62B, CNV 663-73B).

In 1966 Bedford celebrated 800 years of its charter, and Bristol FS6B/ECW 678 (DNV 678C) was given an appropriate livery of all-over cream with dark blue wings and wheels. It ran thus from March to October, being seen outside Bedford depot on 11 June.
Geoff Mills

Bristol SUL4A 304 (JNV 304D) was the penultimate of the type to enter service, in December 1967. This 1968 view shows it climbing Lancot Hill and into Dunstable (despite the destination shown) *en route* from Leighton Buzzard to Luton via Edlesborough. Allocated to Luton, it would not be given a fleet-number plate until 1970.
Chris Lodington

In 1965 came further Bristol FS6B and FLF6B Lodekkas, but no single-deckers were delivered new; those that did appear were six Bristols of 1953/4 vintage — two LS5G buses and four LS6G coaches — acquired from Eastern National. The buses went into service in July, although the coaches — a response to a growth in traffic generated by the M1 motorway — had to wait until the following January. Buses withdrawn in 1965 included Bristol K5Gs, K6Bs and the last LL5Gs to be bought new by United Counties.

The 1966 intake consisted of more Lodekkas — a mixture of FS6Bs, FS6Gs and FLF6Bs — to see off further Bristol Ks. The single-deckers were of more than passing interest, however. The three coaches turned out to be Bristol MWs rather than REs and carried the final style of ECW coach bodywork for the type,

with its distinctive deep windscreens. Nos 260-2 (GRP 260-2D) were the last MWs to be bought new by the company; indeed, the model itself was to bow out the following year. The trio had been bought for the Associated Motorways services linking Cheltenham with Cambridge and Peterborough, although they only seated 39 passengers. Another new type to grace the fleet was the Bristol SU, introduced in 1960 as a replacement for the SC model. Numbered 300-5 (HRP 300-3D, JNV 304/5D), the six for United Counties were 36-seat SUL4A buses. Nos 300-2 were allocated to Northampton for use at Welford, permitting the withdrawal of the modified L5Gs (which themselves had replaced the SCs there) in the summer of 1966, whilst the other three went into store, not emerging until late 1967 (303/4) or early 1968 (305).

Bristol RELH/ECW 263 (KRP 263E) heads towards London on an MX5 journey from Nottingham and Leicester *c*1968. The full journey would take some 4½ hours, including a 17min refreshment stop at Northampton. The equivalent rail journey took just over 2 hours. *Mike Sutcliffe*

UNITED COUNTIES EXPRESS SERVICES

Time and Fare Tables
United Counties Omnibus Co Ltd

In 1967 came the first bus-bodied Bristol REs in the shape of 306-13 (NBD 306-13F), ECW-bodied RELL6Gs, of which 306-10 entered service in November, the remainder being stored until 1968. Further Bristol RELH6G/ECW coaches were 263-70 (KRP 263-70E), whilst the last Bristol Lodekkas to be bought new were FLF6Bs 719-38 (KNV 719-26E, LBD 727-30E, LRP 731-8E). (Of these 735-8 were to have gone to the Scottish Bus Group in exchange for Bristol VRs in 1973, but the deal was cancelled when Scottish Omnibuses discovered the Bristol engine under the bonnet of 736!)

Oddities of 1967 were two Duple-bodied Bedford SBO coaches acquired late in the year from Southern Vectis for rail-replacement duties; not entering service until the following year, 112/3 (ODL 48, 51) were totally non-standard but nevertheless put in some good work until late 1968. Even more non-standard was the Mercedes-Benz O302 integral coach, OLH 302E, demonstrated during April 1967 on the London-Nottingham, running alongside the Bristol RELHs. No orders for this type were forthcoming, but the appearance in Northampton in February of Bristol VR demonstrator HHW 933D presaged the large-scale introduction of the production VRT design.

The Bedford SB was not the sort of vehicle that one would associate with United Counties, but nevertheless two Duple-bodied SBOs joined the fleet, working throughout much of 1968. Retaining its former operator's livery of cream with green trim, 113 (ODL 51) is seen arriving in Northampton, somehow looking less than comfortable in its new role. Sister vehicle 112 (ODL 48) would later work for well-known Derbyshire independent Hulley's of Baslow and was subsequently preserved. *Chris Lodington*

Mercedes-Benz O302 demonstrator OLH 302E waits at Nottingham on the London service in April 1967. Travelling on such a vehicle would have been quite an interesting experience for the passengers, one would imagine; at this time foreign coaches were few and far between on British roads. How times would change! *G. H. F. Atkins / John Banks collection*

A minor acquisition on 2 April 1967 was that of the stage-carriage services of Royal Blue Coach & Transport of Pytchley, consisting of five routes around Kettering. No vehicles were involved in the deal.

The vehicle intake for 1968 included more Bristol RELH6G motorway coaches, 271-6 (ORP 271-6F) and RELL6G buses 314-31 (RBD 314-31G). More interesting perhaps were the second-hand acquisitions, notably the four downgraded Bristol/ECW coaches received from Hants & Dorset; fitted with bus seats, 432-4 (KEL 731-3), LL6Bs new in 1951, and 435 (KRU 996), an LWL6B of similar vintage, worked from Bedford, Kettering and Luton until withdrawal in October.

From October 1968 Birch Bros Ltd, the well-known and long-established independent operator, abandoned its rural routes in Bedfordshire and Hertfordshire, three of which were incorporated into the United Counties network as its 89/123 and 146/147/148. No buses were acquired, and neither was the garage at Henlow Camp; to cover these routes six Bristol LS6G/ECW buses were acquired from Red & White Services, while operation of the 89, which ran from Hitchin to Pirton and Holwell, entailed the creation of an outstation at Holwell.

It should also be mentioned that 1968 was the year that plans were announced for a new city situated in the middle of United Counties' territory, at Milton Keynes.

The year 1969 was a significant one in the history of road passenger transport in the UK, with the formation of the National Bus Company (NBC) from 1 January as a result of the Transport Act 1968. Accordingly ownership of United Counties, comprising all assets and shareholdings, passed from the Transport Holding Company, successor to the British Transport Commission, to the National Bus Company.

The first new buses delivered under the new regime comprised an interesting mix including two new types for the company; 750-7 (RRP 750-3G, TBD 754/5G, UBD 756/7H) were Bristol VRTSL6Gs with 70-seat ECW bodies, and their front-entrance, rear-engined layout must have seemed quite modern to passengers when compared to an FLF and even more so against a Bristol K, a number of which were still in service. The first of this new type were distributed around Stony Stratford, Corby, Wellingborough, Bedford and Aylesbury garages. Also new was the Bristol LH6L/ECW, the first four of which were 400-3 (SRP 400/1G, TBD 402/3G). Further Bristol RELL6Gs were received as 332-45 (SRP 332-6G, UBD 337-42H, URP 343-5H), while there were eight more Bristol RELH6Gs, 277-84 (TBD 277-84G), albeit to dual-purpose rather than coach specification, in order to qualify for Bus Grant; although painted in the cream coach livery, they had bus-shell bodywork fitted with coach seats. The new deliveries saw the demotion of a number of older coaches: four early Bristol RELHs were downgraded to dual-purpose status, whilst a number of Bristol LS and MW coaches received bus seats to allow an increase in one-man operation.

Further retrenchment by Birch Bros saw that operator's London–Rushden service, together with tours and excursion licences from Bedfordshire and Hertfordshire, pass to United Counties with effect from 14 September 1969. Vehicles received were 12 Leyland PSU3 Leopards, the most modern of which were 170-3 (DUC 70-3C) with dual-purpose Marshall bodywork; also dual-purpose were Willowbrook-bodied 182/3 (82/3 CYV), while 190-5 (90-5 FXD) were Park Royal coaches.

Winters aren't what they used to be, at least in Dunstable! In this January 1968 scene Bristol KSW6B/ECW 863 (CNH 702) appears to be making heavy weather of the ascent of Lancot Hill. The photographer, having arrived from finishing a night shift, gave a hand with a shovel before going home to bed! *Chris Lodington*

The company's first Bristol VRs were 750/1 (RRP 750/1G), new in January 1969 and allocated initially to Stony Stratford; seen here in Midland Road, Bedford, working in on a 132, 750 was still based there in May 1977. Upgraded to Series 3 specification in March 1982, this bus would remain with United Counties following the division of the company in 1986. *Chris Lodington*

Unlike their double-deck contemporaries the Bristol L variants failed to make it into NBC ownership in passenger service, all being withdrawn by the end of 1968. The last to be delivered, in May 1952, LWL6B 431 (CNH 865) was not quite the last out, going in May 1968. Since 1957 fitted with a Gardner 5LW engine, it is seen at Stamford, probably near the end, heading towards Market Harborough on the Wednesdays- and Fridays-only 278. *Photobus*

Yet to gain corporate NBC leaf green, Bristol RELL6G/ECW 333 (SRP 333G) waits time in Market Harborough bus station before heading home to Kettering in May 1975. *Chris Lodington*

Demoted to bus status, one-time dual-purpose Bristol RELH6G/ECW 279 (TBD 279G) leaves Dunstable for Hemel Hempstead in April 1982. *Author*

The ex-Birch Leyland Leopards put in several years of good service for their new owners, the last surviving until 1977. Among these would be 172 (DUC 72C), seen taking on what appears to be a full load for Rushden at Bedford in June 1973. Much photographed by enthusiasts over the years, the bus station has served the town for some 45 years, although its days may be numbered, as redevelopment of the area is once again on the cards.
John Aldridge

Bristol LWL5G/ECW 404
(CNH 848) survived to become
a waiting room at Daventry
from 1969, being pictured in
April of that year as Bristol
FS6B/ECW 609 (WBD 609)
arrives on local service 350.
Ian Allan Library

▲ The bus station at Rushden was not acquired, a temporary
waiting room being provided at the town's United Counties
garage in the shape of Bristol KSW5G/ECW 880 (TNO 673).
Indeed, it was quite a time for temporary waiting rooms and the
like; Bristol LS5G 476 (WVX 441) was in position at Luton's
second temporary bus station as a rest room for crews, KSW5G
859 (CNH 698) could be found at the town's Castle Street
garage, where passengers waited for express services diverted
from the bus station, and LWL5G 404 (CNH 848) became a
waiting room at Daventry.

United Counties at the end of 1969 was the very model of an
ex-Tilling fleet. With the exception of the aforementioned

ex-Birch Leyland Leopards (a type that would, ironically,
become the standard NBC coach chassis), all vehicles were of
Bristol manufacture with ECW bodywork. In terms of age
these ranged from recently delivered VRs and REs to a few KS
types that were new back in 1950. The stock taken over from
Eastern National had been all but eliminated, just half a dozen
KSW5Gs surviving into 1970.

As the decade drew to a close, the company was continuing
to return a reasonable profit, but with the onset of the 1970s
the changes shaping the operating industry throughout the
country would have far-reaching effects on the face and fortunes
of the fleet.

4. A National Bus Company

If United Counties represented the archetypal Tilling fleet at the end of 1969 (give or take the odd Leopard), then four days into the new year spoiled all that. On 4 January 1970 the (almost) 21-year-old co-ordination agreement with Luton Corporation Transport came to an end with the takeover of the 82-vehicle fleet. The newest buses in service were 30 ECW-bodied Bristol RELL6Ls dating from 1967-9, which fitted in quite well with the United Counties fleet as 361-90 (MXD 101-5E, NXE 106-10F, PXE 111-20G, UXD 121-30G), although they had Leyland (rather than Gardner) engines and were to dual-door layout. (These were sometimes used on country routes from Luton, on which the driver was able to put his foot down — and how they rattled! At speed it sounded as if someone were kicking around a bag full of cutlery.)

Also inherited were five Bristol LHS6P/ECW saloons (XXE 131-5H), delivered in December 1969; unused by either Luton or United Counties, they passed to Eastern Counties and were re-registered (as WNG 101-5H) before entering service. The 47 double-deckers were a motley collection comprising 23 Leyland PD2s, 16 Albion Lowlanders and eight Dennis Lolines, all of which would be withdrawn by 1974. Most would remain at Luton, although three of the Albions turned up elsewhere in 1972/3, at Aylesbury, Bedford, Corby and Northampton.

The Corporation garage in Kingsway was not retained, all buses being transferred to the United Counties premises in Castle Street in June, by which time the majority of the fleet had been repainted green. By the end of the year all had been so treated, with the exception of several of the oldest Leyland PD2s, which were withdrawn still in the red Luton Corporation livery.

New buses into service in 1970 included more Bristol VR and RE types and a batch of nine Bristol LH6Ls. Ten further Bristol RELLs that had been ordered by Luton Corporation were delivered as 348-57 with Gardner (rather than Leyland) engines; although they bore Northampton registrations (VNV 348-57H) they were identifiable by their dual-door layout.

If anything chracterised the bus industry in the early 'Seventies it was shortages, of staff and vehicles. Industrial relations generally were poor, and as a consequence deliveries of new

buses (and spare parts to keep them going) were vulnerable to strikes or working-to-rule, not to mention the three-day week and, in 1974, the Fuel Crisis. The 'Second-hand 'Seventies', as this period has been dubbed, was a time when many operators had to hire and acquire all sorts of elderly buses to keep services going. United Counties was no exception.

New deliveries for 1971 consisted of nine Bristol RELH6G/ECW dual-purpose vehicles, three RESL6G/ECW buses and four Bristol VRTSL6G/ECW double-deckers, whilst 1972 was no better, bringing five RESL6Gs and 10 VRTSL6Gs.

Second-hand acquisitions for 1971/2 totalled 36, mainly elderly Bristol LD6Gs and LD6Bs from such sources as Lincolnshire Road Car, Notts & Derby, Crosville, Western National and Midland General. The last-named also contributed a trio of Bristol MW6G dual-purpose saloons, whilst from East Yorkshire came five Leyland PSUC1/1 Tiger Cubs. In 1971

The five Bristol LHS6Ps that had been delivered to Luton Corporation just prior to takeover were not retained by United Counties. No 134 (XXE 134H) poses at the Kingsway garage during its short stay in Luton; it would subsequently become Eastern Counties LHS598, re-registered WNG 105H.
Geoff Mills

Still in Luton Corporation red livery on 20 June 1970, 811 (UNM 151), a Metro-Cammell-bodied Leyland PD2/31 new in 1957, bowls along Dallow Road on the frequent service 11, pursued by a youthful cyclist. Painted green the following month, the bus would be withdrawn in 1972. *Bill Fitton*

Looking well turned out in full United Counties livery, 840 (180 HTM) was one of 16 Albion Lowlanders inherited from Luton Corporation on 4 January 1970. Pictured on 20 June in Leagrave High Street, about to turn into Poynters Road on the Luton/Dunstable boundary, it had been repainted two months previously but would be delicensed a week or so later, never to run again for the company. *Bill Fitton*

Amongst the regular intake of vehicles in 1970 were nine dual-purpose Bristol RELH6Gs which differed from the previous year's batch in having curved fronts rather than flat. Delivered in cream, all subsequently received NBC 'local coach' livery of green and white. Having arrived from Milton Keynes, 288 (WBD 288H) is seen at London Victoria on 17 July 1982, during a rail strike; this would explain its appearance, as the type was not usually employed on this service. *Charles Dean / Author's collection*

The last Bristol LH6L saloons for United Counties were the nine delivered in 1971. Biggleswade's 408 (XBD 408J) waits in the sunshine at Bedford in the summer of 1975, working a 180 service back to its home town. The entire batch would pass to Crosville in 1978. *Roy Dixon / Author's collection*

a Dennis Loline was obtained from Aldershot & District in order to provide spares for the ex-Luton buses but proved unsuitable on account of its Gardner (rather than Leyland) engine.

From 1972 NBC dictated that a standard livery style be adopted which, in the case of United Counties, meant leaf green with white relief (for buses), leaf green below the waist with white above (for dual-purpose vehicles) or all-over white (coaches). As United Counties had been a BTC/THC company, its pre-NBC livery was not elaborate, so the change was not that dramatic; indeed, many passengers probably didn't notice at all.

The year 1973 was a much better one for new buses, some 52 new vehicles entering the fleet. Notable was the appearance of the first Leyland National, this type replacing the Bristol RELL

as the company's standard single-deck bus. Also taken into stock, indicating the desperation to buy new buses, were six Willowbrook-bodied Bedford YRQs, the first of many lightweight chassis to grace the fleet; United Counties would turn out to be one of the biggest users of lightweight chassis within NBC. Also taken into stock in 1973 were 25 second-hand buses, of which 16 were Bristol LD6Gs, whilst no fewer than 27 buses were received on hire, including 10 Leyland PSUC1/1 Tiger Cubs from Trent and a trio of AEC Reliances from Maidstone & District.

The period 1970-3 represented the lowest point to be reached by the company, brought about by a combination of lack of investment, problems both within and outside of the industry and

Nine more dual-purpose Bristol RELH6Gs were added in 1971; although full coach bodies were required, these were not available from ECW in that year. This splendid picture of 211 (YRP 211J) was taken at 6.15pm on Sunday 27 June 1971 at Southsea, as the vehicle was leaving Clarence Pier Coach Park to return to Luton; only a month or so old, it had yet to receive a fleet-number plate. The X36 journey took 4hr 20min (including a refreshment break at Bagshot) and in 1971 cost just £1 for a day return or £2 for a period. *Philip Wallis*

Of the many Bristol Lodekkas acquired during the early 1970s, some were better than others. A cut above many was 599 (565 ERR), which came from Mansfield District Traction in 1971; one of the few FS models acquired (most being LDs), and dating only from 1960, it would serve for almost another five years with United Counties, being seen at Luton in May 1972. *Chris Lodington*

UNITED COUNTIES ⟫

Some of the acquired buses were more unusual, demonstrating the desperate measures taken at the time. Problems with recertification of early Bristol LS saloons saw the purchase, from East Yorkshire in 1972, of five Metro-Cammell-bodied Leyland Tiger Cubs. Surrounded by more usual United Counties rolling stock at Bedford on 17 October 1973 is 197 (6684 KH), new in 1960. *Chris Lodington*

poor staff morale; 1970 also had the dubious honour of being the first year in which the company made a loss. However, as the decade progressed there was evidence of a slow recovery; indeed, 1974 was a bumper year for new vehicles, no fewer than 100 entering service, 51 of which were Willowbrook-bodied Bedfords. Along with more Leyland Nationals and Bristol VRs came what would be United Counties' last new Bristol REs; RELH6L models, Leyland engines being fitted in place of the Gardner specified hitherto, 219-23 (SBD 219-23M) would be its only examples to be bodied by Plaxton and although complying with Bus Grant requirements were the company's first new

coaches since ECW-bodied RELH6Gs 271-6 of 1968. Further vehicles were either acquired or hired, the latter including Daimler CVG6s from Northampton, although sadly these were not used in the end.

On the debit side, the early 1970s saw the elimination from the United Counties fleet of several long-established types. The last Bristol KSW6Bs went in 1973, whilst the Bristol LS bowed out during the following year. Even the little Bristol SUL4As were taken out of service in 1973/4. The Bristol LDs were also becoming life-expired, mainly being withdrawn from 1974, although the first (951) had gone in 1970.

Red Bristol RELLs reappeared on the streets of Luton for a short period during 1974 and must have elicited the odd second glance from those recalling similar buses in service with Luton Corporation (the last of which had been painted green late in 1970). West Yorkshire Road Car 1262 (SYG 847F), one of five on loan from that company, is seen in Upper George Street on 21 May, shortly after its arrival with United Counties, working ex-Corporation route 6 to Dunstable via Houghton Regis. *Chris Lodington*

Between 1973 and 1976 United Counties built up an impressive fleet of lightweight Bedford saloons; 193 (GRP 921N) , a Willowbrook-bodied YRQ, basks in the sun at Stamford, Lincolnshire, on 31 May 1975 before running to Edith Weston in Leicestershire, on the northern fringes of United Counties territory. *Chris Lodington*

Numerically United Counties' last Bristol K was 969 (KNV 342), a KSW6B new in October 1954. It soldiered on for nearly 20 years to become (just!) the last of its type in service, in June 1973. Still looking quite presentable, it is seen in Neville Road, Luton, on route 55 a few days before the end. Four KSW6Bs (911/33/4/64) would survive as trainers until 1976.
Bill Fitton

Still in (by now) rather tatty pre-NBC livery, 527 (ORP 27), a Bristol LD6B/ ECW of 1957, works local service 100 in Bedford on 28 May 1975. It would be withdrawn later in the year, so presumably a repaint was never undertaken.
Chris Lodington

◄ A pair of the ex-Court Line Plaxton-bodied Fords at Hemel Hempstead bus station in 1975. Nearer the camera, 202 (YXD 458M), an R1014, heads for Dunstable via Studham as 197 (LXD 433K), an R192, makes for Luton Airport via Markyate. *Geoff Mills*

Timetable
NORTHAMPTON AREA
including Daventry and Buckingham

UNITED COUNTIES

With effect from 9 December 1974 United Counties took over the stage-carriage operations of Court Line Coaches, Luton, together with eight Plaxton-bodied Ford coaches. This company was all that remained following the collapse of Court Line Aviation, and the hope was that it could continue as a separate unit. Bedfordshire County Council was keen to protect its eight services, mainly former London Country routes in the Luton, Dunstable and Hemel Hempstead areas, and operations were conducted initially from the Luton Council depot at Kingsway. Recertification problems saw the use of Bristol LSs until the Fords could be put back into service.

By 1975 deliveries of new buses had settled down and consisted mainly of more Leyland Nationals and Bristol VRs. However, the appearance of half a dozen Deansgate-bodied Mercedes-Benz L406D 15-seaters heralded the first use of dedicated vehicles in Milton Keynes. Carrying a yellow livery, 1-6 (HBD 167-72N) were used initially on a 'dial-a-ride' scheme in Woughton, near to the central area. Although two further

Mercedes — Charterway-bodied O309Ds 7, 8 (MNV 7, 8P) — were bought in 1976, conventional bus services in Milton Keynes were entrusted to full-sized vehicles.

As the decade continued, new vehicle deliveries generally meant more of the same. Single-deck buses were mainly Leyland Nationals, the flirtation with lightweight saloons ending in 1976 with the purchase of 10 Duple-bodied Ford R1014s, 51-60 (OVV 51-60R). More Willowbrook-bodied Bedfords would have been preferred, and the Fords were imposed on United Counties by NBC; all would be withdrawn in 1980. Double-deck deliveries were exclusively Bristol VRs, whilst the company's coaching requirements were catered for by the NBC standard — the Leyland Leopard with either Duple or Plaxton bodywork. If it was variety you were looking for, then from September 1976 a day trip to Leighton Buzzard would find a pair of hired Ford A0609/Tricentrol midibuses on town services, as part of an initiative sponsored by Bedfordshire County Council; painted in dual-purpose livery,

The first truly dedicated vehicles for Milton Keynes were the six Deansgate-bodied Mercedes L406Ds used on a daily 'Dial-a-Ride' service in the Woughton area from March 1975. A lack of space at Bletchley garage saw the operational base established at Wavenden Tower, later moving to another site in Bletchley — formerly occupied by a Co-op bakery — which subsequently became a full garage. They were painted yellow, with the telephone number of the control centre displayed prominently on the side, still retained by 3 (HBD 169N) when photographed at Bletchley on 2 February 1980, not long before the whole batch was sold. *Three Counties Bus & Commercial Vehicle Museum*

Dedicated midibus operation came to Leighton Buzzard and Linslade in September 1976, the five routes being initially worked by a pair of Ford A-series 23-seaters. Supported by Bedfordshire County Council, the initiative soon proved popular with the public; 072 (PKX 272R) stands in the High Street ready to head west towards Weston Avenue. *Three Counties Bus & Commercial Vehicle Museum*

One of five Alexander-bodied Leyland Leopard PSU3C/4RT coaches new in 1976, 228 (MRP 228P) heads away from Victoria Coach Station for layover at Battersea, having arrived in London with passengers from Milton Keynes on 17 July 1982, during that year's national rail strike. *Charles Dean / Author's collection*

they were numbered 071/2 (PKX 271/2R). Also on hire from Ford was Transit 70 (TVD 851R), as transport for the Lilbourne Village Bus, another County Council-sponsored scheme, in this case Northamptonshire; loaned from June 1977, the bus would be acquired by United Counties 10 months later. More interesting, perhaps, was the loan, for several months in 1979, of a pair of Eastern National Bristol FLF/ ECW — 2801 (BVX 677B) and 2928 (AVW 397F) — at Bedford.

The increase in new deliveries was seeing off the Bristol MW and LD (not to mention the last Birch Leopards, in 1977), while the rag-bag of Bristol Lodekkas and saloons that had been acquired earlier in the 1970s had also left the fleet by 1977. Several buses were lost in 1979 as a result of arson; five Bristol REs and a Leyland National were damaged beyond economic repair at Luton garage on 25 February, whilst a number of vehicles awaiting disposal at Wellingborough were destroyed on 26 November, these comprising three ex-Court Line Fords, three ex-Luton Corporation Bristol RELLs and FLF6B 738. We were now at the height of NBC standardisation, which broadly saw a place only for the Leyland National and Leopard and Bristol RE and VR, although numerous Bedford YRTs and YRQs would remain service with United Counties until the early 1980s.

The 1970s saw several new bus stations open to United Counties buses. On 4 January 1970 Aylesbury became the lucky recipient of new premises adjacent to a shopping-centre development and beneath a multi-storey car park. United Counties was the main user, others being City of Oxford, Thames Valley, London Country and local independent Red Rover. It was not a place of beauty. Corby also gained a subterranean edifice, which by all accounts was even worse than that at Aylesbury. Although it was due to open on 3 June 1973, bus crews took strike action instead, in protest over various problems, not least the poorly designed traffic islands that severely impeded access!

'Superider' was an experimental limited-stop service between Luton and Dunstable, running in addition to the normal service. Two Leyland Nationals were fitted with coach-type seats, and a special livery was applied. It was not a success, and the service, which began in December 1976, ceased after only seven months. One of the vehicles, 473 (ORP 473M), retained the Superider livery for a further two years, as apparent from this view recorded at Hemel Hempstead in November 1977. *Geoff Mills*

Another interesting scheme was the introduction of the Lilbourne Community Bus in Northamptonshire, the costs of which were kept down by the use of volunteer drivers trained by United Counties' own instructors. Introduced from 10 June 1977, the service was worked by Ford Transit 70 (TVD 851R), which was hired and later bought by the company. In this early publicity shot the bunting is out — not, one imagines, for the new service but for HM the Queen's Silver Jubilee! *John Aldridge collection*

The 1970s witnessed the gradual development of Milton Keynes, covering an area between Wolverton and Stony Stratford in the north and Bletchley in the south. Services were adapted as the city took shape, with roads laid out on a 'grid' pattern. Initial plans were for a high-frequency flat-fare operation, and there was also talk in the early days of a rapid-transit system and even a monorail, but such ideas ultimately succumbed to a more conventional network. The first indication of a dedicated service had been the appearance, from 1 November 1971, of a couple of dual-purpose Bristol MW6Gs on new route 388 (Bletchley–Stony Stratford–Wolverton); these carried both 'MILTON KEYNES NEW CITY' and 'UNITED COUNTIES' as fleetnames, although the green/cream livery was unchanged. With effect from 19 March 1972 the 388 was renumbered MK1, heralding further 'MK' services. Eventually, on 7 December 1975, in conjunction with major service revisions, a modest open-air bus station was opened at Bletchley, which, with its railway station, at the time was the hub of transport services in Milton Keynes.

On 1 May 1976 the 40-year-old bus station at Derngate, Northampton, closed its doors, to be replaced from the following day by a new one at Greyfriars (also underneath a shopping complex) which was also used by Northampton Transport buses. Derngate was to see a number of other uses, including as a grain store, until its eventual sale at the end of the decade.

And so to Luton. As recounted earlier, the town was on its second 'temporary' bus station, sited between Bridge Street and Williamson Street, as the Arndale shopping centre took shape alongside. The new bus station was built some distance away, in Bute Street, and was to serve as a bus/train interchange, although the railway station was reached via a long (and none too salubrious) footbridge. The bus station, which came into full use on 12 September 1976, was again positioned underneath a multi-storey car park and was as gloomy and depressing as the others.

With effect from 2 April 1978 severe service cuts were implemented in Northamptonshire following a reduction in

▲ In September 1971 Bristol MW6Gs 153/60 (153/60 BRP) were lettered for service in the embryonic 'Milton Keynes New City', as demonstrated by the former at Bletchley in 1972. *Roy Dixon / Author's collection*

financial support from the County Council. In a leaflet issued
by United Counties it was stated that a million passenger miles
would be lost and that the garages at Daventry, Desborough and
Rushden would have to close. The cuts also resulted in many
redundancies (fortunately all voluntary), as well as a reduction
in the number of buses required; among the vehicular casualties
were the unloved Bristol LH saloons, all of which headed north
for further use with Crosville.

On a more positive note, the summer of 1979 saw the launch
of the Milton Keynes 'Citybus' network (and logo), at around
the same time as the opening of the large shopping centre in
central Milton Keynes. Although vinyls were applied to all
vehicles operating from Stony Stratford and Bletchley depots,
the lack of a distinctive livery for the city fleet, which consisted
mainly of Bristol VRs, REs and FLFs, together with Leyland
Nationals, rather lessened the impact. New ticketing initiatives
were also introduced, to encourage potential shoppers to travel
by bus. By the 1980s a new depot was required for the fleet of
buses used on city services and this was opened at Winterhill on

27 May 1983, replacing both Bletchley and Stony Stratford, and
bearing the colour code of green and black. On the same day
a new bus station was opened in Milton Keynes. Situated a mile
from the shops, it was inconveniently sited and consequently
always under-used, although, as in Luton, it was more convenient
for the railway station, which had opened a year previously.

There was some integration to note, although the experience
was not always a happy one; a dedicated service from rail-less
Corby to Kettering, marketed as 'Corby Link' and operated
from 22 November 1976 to 1 April 1978 using blue-and-white-
liveried Bristol RELH6G 217, was not a success. On 12 May
1980 another service was introduced, this linking Kettering
(on the Midland main line) and Peterborough (on the East Coast
main line) by way of Corby and Oundle (both off the British Rail
network), using two dedicated Leyland Leopards, 242/3
(MRP 242/3V), painted blue and grey; again, loadings were
never sufficient to justify provision of the service, which,
following reductions in frequency, would be withdrawn exactly
four years after it had started.

Corby, one of the largest towns in the country without the benefit of a railway station (along with Mansfield and, apparently, Dunstable), was chosen for the experiment of a dedicated rail link with Kettering, promoted as 'Corby Link' and run in addition to the regular bus services. Painted in a special livery of blue and white, Bristol RELH6G 217 (KRP 217L) awaits custom at Kettering three days into the new service, on 25 November 1976. Regrettably the service would not prove a success, running only until 1 April 1978. A rail service would be restored in April 1987, but this too would cease after three years. *Chris Lodington*

Another Rail Link provided by United Counties was that between Kettering and Peterborough via Corby and Oundle, introduced in May 1980. Painted in a slightly modified livery of Rail blue and grey, 242 (MRP 242V), a Leyland Leopard with Plaxton Supreme IV bodywork, was one of two such vehicles dedicated to the service. *British Rail*

A view inside the Central Repair Works at Northampton in April 1984, with a pair of ex-London Country Green Line AEC Reliance coaches (RS36 and RB49) undergoing refurbishment. Beyond are two Bristol VRs receiving major repairs. *Author*

In 1983/4 facilities at the Central Repair Works at Northampton benefited from a significant upgrading, a by-product of which was the ability to take on repair and other work from outside United Counties. For example, a large number of ex-London Country RB- and RS-class AEC Reliance Green Line coaches were refurbished prior to their return to the lessor, Kirby, for resale. Repair work was also undertaken for other NBC subsidiaries such as Midland Fox. A visit by the author in April 1984 revealed all this activity, together with repairs to the company's own vehicles, not to mention the ongoing programme of upgrading Bristol VRs to Series 3 specification — all in all a busy time! From this, United Counties Engineering, a new limited company, was formed from 8 September 1985, to develop these activities.

In the early 1980s Luton was the scene of competition from local firm Three Star Taxis, trading as Lunar Module, which had proposed a minibus service in the town. Despite fierce opposition from United Counties, which saw it as creaming off short-distance passengers, and prolonged negotiations with the Traffic Commissioners, the service got underway on 11 May 1984 and was promoted as 'Lutonian'. Talbot Express minibuses were employed and a flat fare of 10p (upped to 15p before the end of the year) was charged.

New-vehicle deliveries for the period 1980-5 were quite conservative. Double-deckers consisted of more ECW-bodied Bristol VRs, the last entering service in June 1981, to be followed later in the year by ECW-bodied Leyland Olympians. Full-size saloons were limited to 10 Leyland National 2s,

United Counties bought 10 examples of the Leyland National 2
in 1980/1, these representing the last full-sized saloons delivered
before the break-up of the company. Pictured almost brand-new
at Milton Keynes on 30 May 1980, 583 (NRP 583V) looks rather
drab without the white waistband that would be applied
subsequently. *Chris Lodington*

whilst smaller single-deckers were a trio of Lex-bodied Bedford YMQ/S 33-seaters for Leighton Buzzard town services. New Ford Transit minibuses were obtained for Lilbourne and Rushden community services, but, more significantly, in 1985 seven Ford Transit minibuses were introduced on a route in Luton. Although they were delivered earlier in the year, the service did not commence until 1 December and thus operated for only a month before being transferred to Luton & District Transport. All other new vehicles were coaches, Leyland Leopards with bodywork by Willowbrook, Duple or ECW being followed from 1983 by Plaxton-bodied Leyland Tigers. The handful of acquired vehicles were further Leopards, from National Travel (West) and Trent, and a pair of 1973-vintage Bristol VRs from West Riding, the latter entering service at Huntingdon in 1985.

Notable withdrawals were the last Bristol Lodekkas in the fleet, the final survivors — rear-entrance FS types — running from Luton until service revisions implemented on 2 November 1980 brought an end to crew operation. Several of these buses survived in the service fleet. Less mourned were the last of the lightweight saloons delivered in the 1970s, the final Willowbrook-bodied Bedfords departing the fleet in 1981.

The 1980s saw a relaxation of the NBC corporate image, starting on a small scale in 1981, when a quartet of Bristol VRs appeared in a version of the Wellingborough Motor Omnibus (and early United Counties) livery to commemorate 60 years since the formation of United Counties itself. From 1983 some coaches received an orange, green and white 'local coach' scheme (which was not as bad as it sounds!), whilst a trio of high-floor Plaxton-bodied Leyland Tigers delivered in 1985 received an attractive scheme of two-tone metallic blue and white for private-hire work.

Leighton Buzzard town services were given a boost in May 1981 following the introduction of the three 33-seat Lex-bodied Bedford YMQ/S midibuses. No 52 (WNH 52W) waits in the High Street when new, although the use of a slipboard in the windscreen does tend to spoil the image a little. *Author*

In 1984/5 two Bristol REs were painted yellow with green lettering to promote road safety. One of these (the other being RELH 212) was Luton's RELL6G 344 (URP 344H), seen here in Dunstable in October 1985; it passed to Luton & District in 1986 and following withdrawal in 1987 became a mobile café near Harlington, still in yellow livery. *Author*

Amongst the large numbers of coaches delivered during the late 1970s and early 1980s were 10 Willowbrook-bodied Leyland Leopards new in 1980/1; 241 (KVV 241V) passes through Dunstable *en route* from Milton Keynes to London Victoria in August 1981. *Author*

The last coaches to be delivered to
United Counties before the break-up
of the company were a trio of well-
appointed Plaxton Paramount
3500-bodied Leyland Tigers,
81-3 (81 CBK, 82 LUP, 83 CBD).
These brought to a conclusion four
years of coach-buying that injected
66 new vehicles into the fleet.
The blue and white livery was a
departure from the norm, and they
were marketed as 'Executive
Coaches', while the style of fleetname
was perpetuated by United Counties
after 1986. Seen receiving a wash and
brush-up at Luton in October 1985,
81 subsequently passed to Luton
& District Transport; 82 went to
Milton Keynes City Bus, while 83
remained with United Counties.
Author

The last buses to enter the fleet
in 1985 were seven Carlyle-
bodied Ford Transit minibuses
for Luton, 21-7 (C21-6 NVV,
B27 HRP). Only 27 was
licensed before 1 August,
being loaned to Devon General,
hence its 'B' registration.
No 23 climbs into town along
Dunstable Road just prior to
Christmas, a week or so before
transfer to Luton & District.
Author

Following the break-up Luton & District chose arguably the better livery style, although, living in the area, the author may just be biased! The red and ivory colours chosen were most attractive; seen in Luton, both apparently fresh from the paintshop, are Bristol VRs 957 (VVV 957W) and 917 (RTH 917S), the latter new to South Wales Transport. *Author*

5. Getting up to Date

As a prelude to privatisation United Counties was split into three operating companies with effect from 1 January 1986. Luton & District Transport Co Ltd, with garages at Luton, Hitchin, Aylesbury, Leighton Buzzard and Toddington, began with a fleet of 193 vehicles, whilst Milton Keynes City Bus Ltd, with the new depot at Winterhill, took 64 vehicles. United Counties therefore entered 1986 with just 263 buses and coaches — fewer than the 297 owned before the transfer in 1952 of Eastern National's Midland Area. The reduced fleet consisted of the familiar mix of Bristol VR and Leyland Olympian double-deckers, Leyland Nationals, surviving Bristol REs of various types, and Leyland Leopards and Tigers. It retained garages at Northampton, Kettering, Corby, Wellingborough, Bedford, Biggleswade and Huntingdon. Subsequent developments saw the closure of the depot at Wellingborough and the transfer (in a complicated deal in May 1997) to MK Metro of the Huntingdon

operations. Biggleswade garage was also closed, and the site sold for redevelopment in 1989, United Counties moving into the former Charles Cook premises in the town, this depot later being downgraded to an outstation to Bedford.

Although the 'glory days' (however one defines them) are now over, the company continues to operate throughout Northamptonshire and north Bedfordshire, and the past 20 years have not been without interest for the enthusiast. An early change, for example, was the introduction from May 1986 of a network of limited-stop routes marketed under the 'Coachlink' brand, coaches wearing a new livery of white, blue-grey and black. The first minibus network (excluding that at Luton, which was lost with the break-up) was introduced as 'Street Shuttle' at St Neots in October 1986, subsequent operations taking in Kettering, Bedford, Wellingborough, Daventry and Corby.

The National Bus Company was required to dispose of its

▲ Milton Keynes City Bus introduced a rather insipid variety of white or grey, depending upon vehicle type. Although the inherited fleet consisted mainly of Bristol VRs and Leyland Nationals, deregulation saw the introduction *en masse* of minibuses; from 26 October 1986 most services were in the hands of no fewer than 92 Mercedes-Benz L608Ds, in one of the biggest conversions nationwide in what was arguably 'the year of the minibus'. This scene at Bletchley bus station is typical of the period. *Author*

Following sale by United Counties in March 1957 Leyland Titan TD5 572 (FEV 178) passed to operators in London and Yorkshire and later passed into preservation. Acquired by the new Luton & District company in 1987, it was painted into the livery of Luton Corporation (which, of course, it never carried) by apprentices at Castle Street garage, it was once allocated, being seen here in April 1991. It would be sold following the takeover by Arriva and is now privately preserved. *Author*

The new United Counties colour scheme was also quite pleasing, consisting of dark green with orange, yellow and cream stripes. It is seen here to good effect on Leyland National 465 (ORP 465M), at work in Northampton in May 1987. *Chris Lodington*

subsidiaries by 1989. Luton & District was bought by its management and employees in August 1987, whilst Milton Keynes City Bus was subject to a management buy-out in the same month. The management of United Counties lost out to a successful bid for the company by Stagecoach, then a relative newcomer with only two other former NBC subsidiaries, the deal being completed on 18 November 1987.

An early manifestation of the new regime was the introduction of former London Transport AEC Routemasters on town services in Bedford and Corby in January and February 1988

respectively — a move popular with passengers (and enthusiasts). Extensive use was made of '*Routemaster*' branding, this being applied both to vehicles and to publicity material. However, all good things come to an end; Routemaster operations at Corby ceased on 30 August 1991 and those at Bedford on 6 September 1993, whereafter a few of the buses were repainted from United Counties green into Stagecoach corporate livery to form a reserve fleet to counter competition should it arise elsewhere in the country. Former London Transport buses returned to Corby in 1998/9 in the shape of

The Routemasters also looked good in the new scheme; 713 (224 CLT), formerly RM1224, works route 1 in Corby in June 1990. The operation of Routemasters (and the minibuses that later replaced them) was a bid to counter the extensive use of taxis, several of which are visible in the background. *Author*

All-over advertising buses have brightened up many a fleet over the years, including that of United Counties. In this view, chosen as much for the location as for the bus, Bristol VRT 721 (LFJ 862W) poses at Lavenham before heading for Bletchley in June 1990. New to Devon General, it promoted the Royal British Legion for nine years, from 1989 to 1998. *Author*

Leyland Titans cascaded from East London or Selkent, but all had gone by 2004. The fleet in mid-2005 totals 338 vehicles, including eleven driver trainers. Double-deckers are mainly Leyland and Volvo Olympians but also include Dennis Tridents (at Kettering) and Scanias (at Corby). Single-deckers are all Dennis Darts, whilst there are also Optare Solo and Mercedes 709D minibuses. The coach fleet consists of Volvo B10Ms. Two Bristol FLFs originally with Eastern Counties, one now open-top, form a heritage fleet.

The United Counties name has naturally been prominent on the sides of buses and on publicity since 1921, but following restructuring of Stagecoach's UK Bus division, whereby companies have been put into regional groupings (United Counties being included in Stagecoach East, along with Cambus at Cambridge and Viscount at Peterborough), and the introduction of a new corporate identity buses and publicity now identify only the area of operation, such as 'Stagecoach in Bedford'. However, although use of its title is confined (on vehicles, at least) to the legal lettering, the United Counties Omnibus Co, based at Rothersthorpe Avenue, Northampton, remains the principal operator of bus services in Northamptonshire and north Bedfordshire — a situation which looks set to continue for the foreseeable future.

The sale of the company to Stagecoach in November 1987 would eventually see the introduction of that group's corporate image. The now familiar white-with-stripes livery made quite an impact at the time, although in retrospect the individuality of the green is much missed. However, the early Stagecoach livery incorporated a large *UNITED COUNTIES* fleetname as prominent as it had been before the war. Pictured here is 401 (L401 JBD), first of 21 Alexander Dash-bodied Volvo B6s introduced on revamped Bedford town services from 6 September 1993, replacing *inter alia* the Routemaster fleet. Photographed during the first week of the revised service, it is loading in Midland Road, an area since pedestrianised.
Author

With the introduction, from 1994, of a new Stagecoach fleetname, the operating subsidiary's name appeared underneath in smaller lettering and was virtually illegible at even a modest distance. Northern Counties-bodied Leyland Olympian 664 (K664 UNH), one of 15 delivered in 1992, leaves Dunstable, deep in Luton & District territory, for Bedford in April 1995. This unremunerative route survives with Stagecoach despite severe cuts in 2004.
Author

The United Counties fleet continues to evolve, with the Stagecoach corporate image being abandoned in favour of local schemes where appropriate. The 'Corby Star' operations feature an orange, red and yellow livery, seen here on Optare Solo 47037 (KX03 KZB) in Dunedin Road, Corby, on 22 April 2005.
G. B. Wise

A number of former United Counties buses survive in preservation, several of which have already received a mention in the preceding pages. A Bristol Lodekka FS6G dating from 1966, 712 (KBD 712D) was amongst the last in service and is seen taking part in the Luton Festival of Transport, shuttling between Stockwood Park and the town centre, in June 1994. *Author*

Bibliography

British Buses since 1945 by Stephen Morris (Ian Allan Publishing, 1995)

Bus Kaleidoscope 1948 by Philip Wallis (Ian Allan Publishing, 1998)

Buses Annual 1977, edited by Gavin Booth (Ian Allan, 1976)

Glory Days: Eastern National by Richard Delahoy (Ian Allan Publishing, 2003)

The Leyland Man by Mike A. Sutcliffe (Crowood Press, 2003)

National Bus Company — The Early Years by Kevin Lane (Ian Allan Publishing, 2004)

Northampton: Images of Wartime by Alan Burnham (Jones-Sands, 1994)

Routemaster Handbook by Andrew Morgan (Capital Transport, 1992)

The Years Between, Volume 2: The Eastern National Story from 1930 to 1969 by R. J. Crawley, D. R. MacGregor and F. D. Simpson (Oxford Publishing Co, 1984)

Various issues of *Buses, Buses Extra, Preserved Bus* and *Bus & Coach Preservation* (Ian Allan Publishing), *Classic Bus* (Classic Bus Publishing)

Much use has also been made of the invaluable series of books covering the history of United Counties (and Wellingborough Motor Omnibus Co) up until 1999, written and published by Roger Warwick; details can be supplied by the author at 'Torestyn', 101 Broadway East, Northampton NN3 2PP.